QH
166
S8
1975b

Sturla Fridriksson

Surtsey

Date Due

35376 -2

SURTSEY

Frontispiece: An aerial view of Surtsey, summer 1973

SURTSEY

STURLA FRIDRIKSSON

A HALSTED PRESS BOOK

JOHN WILEY & SONS
New York · Toronto

Published in the U.S.A. and
Canada by Halsted Press,
a Division of John Wiley &
Sons, Inc., New York

ISBN 0 470 28000 X

Library of Congress Catalog
Card No. 74–30850

© Butterworths 1975

First Published 1975

Printed in England by Cox
& Wyman Ltd. London, Fakenham
and Reading

PREFACE

This book about Surtsey describes the exceptional event that took place when the sea started to boil off the Icelandic coast. It gives an account of the volcanic eruption that began on the ocean floor in 1963, and of the formation of the island that at the time attracted worldwide attention. The eruption was truly a magnificent phenomenon, with which little else can be compared. It lasted for over three and a half years, and it was naturally a wonderful sight for the many tourists who stop over at Keflavik International Airport in Iceland on trans-Atlantic flights.

Of course, I followed the progress of the eruption and the building up of the island with great interest, but I also waited eagerly for the time when the fires would subside and the surface of the island begin to cool down. It could be foreseen that a unique opportunity for biological research would here present itself, which would be no less interesting than the history of the formation of the island itself, though the former might be slower and less spectacular when compared with the grandeur of the geological story.

Admittedly, it is possible to study some aspects of colonisation by putting out buoys or rafts and then waiting until some form of life establishes itself there. It also happens that when sandspits form in estuaries, the invasion of life may be observed. But here something quite different and much greater had happened: a whole island had been created, and an extensive area of land had been formed from the primary rock. From the depths of the ocean there had been built up a broad base, on the top of which was an island with mountains and craters, lava flows, cliffs, gentle slopes, flat sandy beaches and withered coastal strips with worn, rounded pebbles and boulder rims that gave the landscape an ancient appearance. Surtsey had thus a diversity of topographical features and a variety of substrates in marine and terrestrial habitats.

Although Surtsey was way out in the ocean, it was not long before various living organisms began to appear on the island. Some of these happened to fall into a favourable substrate and consequently succeeded in establishing themselves. All such events were recorded as they occurred, and one could be sure that a trip to the island would always reveal something new of interest to a biologist.

When walking along the coast of the virgin island, it was an amazing sight to see the first leaves of a sprouting seedling like a small green star on the black basaltic sand—the first higher plant to commence growth on this great island. Similarly, it was a great event during an expedition in 1967 when a group of scientists discovered the first flowering plant. The following observation was expressed by one of the participants, Dr. John Marr of Colorado University:

Walking on newborn land of dust and rocks fresh from the earth's interior is not just another conference field trip. Geologists risking burned noses while bending over the edge of a small crater to get a glimpse of our planet's ultra-boiling inside, and botanists huddled down on wet volcanic beach sand in cold rain to see the first plant to flower on the earth's newest mountain are living the thrills that drive field scientists abroad in search of new facts, new ideas and unique experiences.

People have trudged up the track trodden out in the loose cinders, ascending the hill above the research hut, in order to obtain a good overall view of the spouting craters and the rough expanse of lava. Traversing this lava was slow, difficult and dangerous. There were cracking noises when the newly congealed surface of the lava crust gave way below one's feet, and red-hot magma could be seen glowing in the crevices. It was not advisable to remain long in the same spot, for the soles of one's boots soon started to smoulder, and if a rucksack was carelessly left behind it might start to melt in the uprush of hot air. Bluish vapour arose from the craters, while glowing lava and Pele's hairs were whirled up from the magma mass when the wind swept across the crater openings. But these same air currents, which blew light pumice around and scoured the mountain cones, also carried spores and feathered seed from the mainland that became stuck in the rough surface of the lava. And one day there suddenly appeared a thin green cover on the black lava—the first moss plants had conquered the newly moulded glassy surface of the rock.

At the same time as the magma poured into the ocean, building up the lava layers one on top of the other, the waves were slicing from the latter enormous blocks that were back-folded upon the edge of the cliff and with fantastic power moving them hundreds of metres along the shore, polishing them into rounded boulders and stacking them up on the leeward side. Sheltered by these, seaweed and seed of coastal plants were washed ashore: the first invaders of life on this newly formed volcanic terrace. The powerful pounding of the ocean waves continually broke the rock and carved high cliffs into the lava edge, and during one spring a few sea-birds found the ledges of these cliffs an ideal place for laying eggs and rearing their young. In this way the forces of destruction and construction balance one another, while the cold, barren surface of the island is gradually transformed into teeming life with green areas of vegetation, swarms of flies and flocks of birds.

Although studies of the life on the island are being steadily continued, they are subject to the whims of the weather. Landing on the island has often been difficult and, although the rubber dinghies powered by outboard motors are excellent vehicles, they have frequently come to grief in the surf barrier. Cameras and various items of research equipment have fallen into the sea, and many a scientists has had a chilly ducking. The sandy terrace has also proved a poor landing-strip for the single-engined plane used for transportation purposes. During spells of bad weather there has been no connection at all with the mainland. Yet despite these and other difficulties, scientists have met the challenge and stayed for short or long periods in order to satisfy their curiosity and to trace the history of the development of life on this remote island.

Sturla Friðþjófsson

CONTENTS

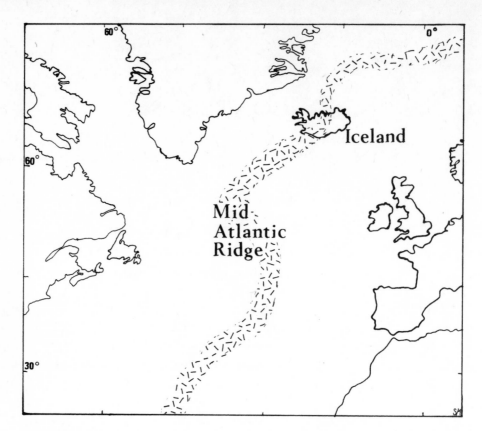

60°   0°

Iceland

60°

Mid
Atlantic
Ridge

30°

SM

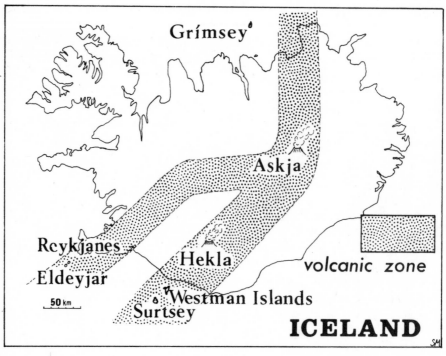

Grímsey

Askja

Reykjanes

Hekla

Eldeyjar

volcanic zone

50 km

Westman Islands

Surtsey

ICELAND

SM

I

INTRODUCTION

A biological study on a volcanic island, which was piled up from the ocean floor by showers of black ash and cinder and by streams of glowing lava in the North Atlantic off the shores of Iceland with its glaciers of eternal ice towering in the background as a contrast to the smoking island, leads one's thoughts to the dawn of life, to the range life is given between the boundaries of cold and heat, and to the fate of life.

In the heathen religion of the old Norsemen, the ancestors of modern Icelanders, life was thought to have originated as the ooze from the cold world of Niflheimur met with the hot mist from the world of Muspellsheimur. In the beginning was only chaos, as there was yet no Heaven or Earth. In the North was a region of snow and ice, and in the South there was heat and fire. And in the yawning gap between these regions, life arose. It was born out of the elements, and although at first hardly to be distinguished from the non-living, it developed into the complex forms of life, with its plants and animals, including man. In the poem *Völuspá*, which was probably written in Iceland in the middle of the tenth century, the birth of life and its fate is described by Vala, the wandering prophetess. She tells Odin, the chief of the gods, about the past, of the creation of the world, about the first man and woman, about the tree of life, Yggdrasill:

'Of old was the age when Ymir lived,
Sea nor cool waves nor sand there were
Earth had not been, nor Heaven above,
but a yawning gap, and grass nowhere.'

And as life later developed and prospered on earth, it was in the end destroyed by the giant who possessed the fire. The name of this mythical fire-giant was Surtur, the Black:

'Surtur fares from the South
with the scourge of branches,
the sun turns black,
earth sinks in the sea.
The hot stars down
from Heaven are whirled.
Fierce grows the steam
and the life-feeding flame.
Till fire leaps high
about Heaven itself.'

In Iceland the Norsemen became acquainted with volcanic activity, which they undoubtedly connected with the actions of the fire-giant. This power was later inherited by another evil spirit with the advent of Christianity, as in the Middle Ages one of the greatest and most active Icelandic volcanoes, Mt Hekla, was believed to be the main entrance to Hell.

When in 1963 fires started burning from the bottom of the ocean and building up a cone of cinders, it was not surprising that the island formed should be named Surtsey, the island of the fire-giant Surtur.

As it was foreseen, in the spring of 1964, that the island would survive the destructive forces of the ocean, it started to awaken interest among biologists.

In the biological studies on Surtsey, the scientists are dealing with the uttermost outposts of life. They can study how life can disperse and develop on the barren and dry lava and beside the boiling vapours of the fissures and vents in the surface of Surtsey. And they can compare this with the development of life on nunataks, barren peaks protruding from the eternal ice, or on barren patches of land recently freed from the receding glaciers. These contrasts are met with in Iceland, and within this frame is the topic of the Surtsey scientists.

It is not every day that a new volcanic island is born, and it is a rather unique event for scientists to have the opportunity to witness the labour of Mother Earth and to be allowed to watch Nature as midwife dress the new-born with the garments and ornaments of Flora and Fauna.

During the history of man, it is known that only a few volcanic islands have been formed. But these events have not been utilised for a thorough and continuous scientific study. Even on Krakatoa, which erupted in 1883, little is known about the first steps in the colonisation of its biota. The first botanist visited the island only three years after the eruption occurred, finding then over 30 species of plants. Ten years later the island was covered with vegetation, predominantly savanna and isolated shrubs. On Krakatoa there was no investigation as to the kind of habitat in which each species lived and in what frequency it occurred. Compared with the luxurious vegetation and animal life of the Indonesian neighbourhood of Krakatoa with its favourable climate for development of the various life forms, Surtsey is situated in rather barren surroundings with a harsh climate and hostile growth conditions. All developments are therefore rather slow. And Nature's effort to bring her garments to the island from her rather poor supply is repeatedly hindered.

Surtsey is the outermost of a group of islands. It is subjected to strong winds that blow ash and pumice back and forth over the surface, scouring away the attempts of any bold colonist. The Atlantic waves constantly pound on the pedestal, erode the shoreline and pour showers of brine over the surface. And in addition, new volcanoes have repeatedly erupted new lava and ashes over the island, destroying the life already established there.

The colonisation is thus like a slow-motion picture which can be followed in detail, but Nature has all the time she needs for doing the job, which she will eventually succeed in doing, and Nature is in no hurry to have this task completed.

The eruption that started on 14 November 1963 in the ocean south of the Westman Islands off the coast of Iceland gradually built up an island which attained a height of 172 m and an area of 2.5 sq. km. Half of the area is now covered with lava, the remainder being mostly ashes which will harden into tuff, while, in places, the beach consists of sand and gravel. The geologists carefully watched the island in the making, and it is through them that we know that during lulls in the early phases of the eruption sea-gulls came to rest on the warm cinder cone of the newly born island.

The first life forms to invade Surtsey were undoubtedly various micro-organisms carried by air and ocean.

My first visit to the island took place on 14 May 1964, six months after the eruption started, at which time various strains of bacteria and a few moulds were collected on agar plates, one fly (*Diamesa zeryni*) was found, while a few sea-gulls, waders and a snow bunting were seen. In addition, a few plant parts and seeds of various beach and sand plants had drifted upon the eastern shore of the island. Since then records of the colonisation of the dry-land biota have been made at short or longer intervals. During the summer months regular observations have been made, but these have been less frequent or completely suspended during the winter months, especially as

3

landing on the island is extremely difficult even in summer, and when winter sets in all biological activities in general are at a minimum in these northern regions.

THE SURTSEY RESEARCH SOCIETY

Shortly after the island was formed and living organisms were discovered on Surtsey, it became obvious that interested scientists would have to get together and organise their research on Surtsey. An excursion to the island was a major undertaking, as it was necessary to use large vehicles, aircraft and ships with special equipment for landing on the island. The cost of this was prohibitive, unless people travelled in groups. It was also essential to establish a centre which could aid foreign scientists and assist in the arrangement of trips to the island. It also became necessary to collect results of research for publication. For these reasons, the Surtsey Research Society was established.

In the by-laws of the Society, the main objectives are outlined as follows:

> The purpose of the Society is to promote research in the geological and biological sciences in connection with the island of Surtsey, and in Iceland in general. The Society itself shall not undertake scientific research work, but shall endeavour to promote and co-ordinate scientific research in the field of geological and biological sciences.

The Society has from the beginning rendered valuable service by acting as a centre for Surtsey research. It publishes the annual results of the scientific research undertaken on the island in the proceedings of the Society. The Surtsey Research Society was responsible for the erection of a small hut on the island with a laboratory, which scientists can use during their excursion trips. In this hut, one or two students of natural science have been permanently stationed during the summer months. They make various daily recordings, in addition to acting as guardians of the island.

CONSERVATION MEASURES

Surtsey was a unique geological phenomenon, and at the same time it became a biological laboratory. But in order to study the sequence of events on the island, it was essential that man himself should influence the ecosystem as little as possible. It was realised that visitors had to be particularly careful not to engage in any activity that would affect natural dispersal of living organisms to the island, or that would in any way alter the habitat and the life on the island. Thus it was obvious that, if the living processes were to be studied on Surtsey, restrictions would have to be placed on the movements of visitors to the island.

This was a rather controversial point, as the island is a great tourist attraction. Nevertheless, Surtsey was declared a protected area for the sake of science. And tourists have not had access to the island. In the hut at Surtsey the regulations for visitors include the following items:

> This hut is the joint property of the Surtsey Research Society, the Life Saving Society of the Westman Islands and the Icelandic Accident Prevention Association.
>
> Visitors are welcome, but are asked to bear in mind that the hut is not only a shelter for the shipwrecked, but also a centre for important scientific research, both geological and biological; actually this also applies to the whole island of Surtsey. It is therefore highly important that all rules be strictly adhered to.
>
> 1. On arrival at the island please carefully avoid bringing with you any soil or pollutants.
> 2. Please leave outer clothing or foot-wear in the entrance.
> 3. Please leave all your food in the hut and have your meals indoors.
> 4. Please do not leave any organic wastes outside or inside the hut.
> 5. Please bury or burn all left-overs, or take them along with you when leaving the island.
> 6. Please use the toilet in the hut and carefully observe all instructions for use.
> 7. Please be careful when handling fire.
> 8. As little movement and disturbance of Nature as possible on the island is requested.
>
> Please bear in mind that Surtsey is protected by law in accordance with a decision of the Nature Protection Council and is under the control of the Surtsey Research Society. The results of the research work done on the island might become of outstanding value and could greatly expand man's knowledge of various developments in Nature.
>
> This requires the cooperation and goodwill of all visitors.
>
> *The Surtsey Research Society*

It was realised that a number of biologists were interested in the Surtsey research. Specialists had to be contacted in order to cover the various fields of biological sciences, and co-ordination of research was needed. This was arranged by the Surtsey Research Society and its scientific members.

In the autumn of 1964, the Surtsey Research Committee (which was the forerunner of the Society) drew up a priority programme for all the Surtsey research. It was a plan for a one-and-a-half year period, commencing in the spring of 1964.

It was suggested that the oceanographic and marine biological research should be handled by scientists from the Department of Fisheries, the University Research Institute, both during their regular trips to the fishing grounds around Surtsey as well as during special trips to the island.

Regarding terrestrial biology, it was realised that the study of the colonisation of the fauna would furnish valuable information about its succession, especially the spreading potential of various groups of invertebrates, but that it would be a study which would have to be continued for a long time and would require the co-operative work of specialists in various fields of invertebrate zoology. It was indicated that special attention should be paid to ornithological studies and the role of birds in transporting other life forms to the island.

Regarding the study of the terrestrial flora, emphasis should be placed on the dispersal of plants, as rather little is known about the dispersal over sea and by ocean in these northern latitudes. It was realised that Surtsey provided a special opportunity for the study of plant succession from the very first stages. This was also regarded as a long-term project.

The studies were continued in the spring of 1964 and in February 1965. The results from those studies were published in the first progress report of the Society, in which a summary was given of the marine biological survey around and on Surtsey, describing the results of several benthonic and plankton samples taken at various times in the waters around Surtsey. A list of a few marine animals which had drifted ashore on Surtsey on 25 November 1964 appeared in the report. It was concluded that the marine biological survey indicated that the eruption had not affected life in the sea around Surtsey, except for the benthonic animals in the area covered by a thick layer of volcanic material. At that time no macroscopic plants had been observed growing on the coast of Surtsey, with the single exception of a filamentous *Chlorophyceae* species, which was found forming small mats on a piece of wood that had drifted ashore. In my report at that time, the general factors affecting the colonisation of the microbial flora were mentioned. There were no signs of mosses, lichens or vascular plants growing on the island, but it was stressed that Surtsey would provide an excellent opportunity for the study of the spreading potential of various life forms and their means of transport. By knowing the biota of other habitats adjacent to Surtsey, it would, for example, be possible to determine the minimal distance a given species would have had to travel in order to reach the new island.

It was pointed out that, as Surtsey was the southernmost part of Iceland, it was quite possible that migrating birds from the continent of Europe would land there first after flight across the ocean. And that it might be possible to detect to what extent birds take part in the transport of the biota across the Atlantic Ocean.

In the spring of 1965 the Surtsey Research Committee organised a more extensive programme of biological research on Surtsey and its environment. A detailed project was prepared, listing various fields of biological work that could be studied on Surtsey. It was also pointed out that, concurrently with the biological work, it would be necessary to study the development of soil on Surtsey in comparison with selected areas on the mainland. It would also be essential to carry out micro-climatological recording on the island.

Although the research on Surtsey was regarded as of primary importance, it was realised that it would be valuable to compare the island with the adjacent islands and certain areas on the mainland, including lava flows of different ages and nunataks, which are mountain peaks isolated by glacial ice just as Surtsey has the ocean as the ecological barrier.

This programme was presented at a conference sponsored by the Society and held in Reykjavik, 27–29 May 1965, where 38 scientists, 22 of whom were Icelandic, got together for the purpose of discussing the programme and to advise on the feasibility of undertaking an extensive biological study. The various reports, discussions and recommendations of the sub-committees, were published in the proceedings of the Surtsey Biology Conference 1965. The groups all recommended that a more extensive programme should be carried out, indicated various priority programmes, and encouraged the use of this rare opportunity for biological studies offered by Surtsey.

In the summer of 1965 the biological study thus became more extensive, and several additional scientists took part in the research work.

During the first 10 years following the eruption, the biological studies were performed according to the programme originally planned, except for occasional slight alterations.

THE SCIENTISTS

A group of Icelandic scientists forms the nucleus of the Surtsey research team. They have organised most of the data collection and the various recordings performed regularly by the guardians and students stationed on the island. However, experts from other countries were also invited to take part in specific studies. Various grants enabled the Surtsey Research Society to obtain the services of competent foreign experts for those research tasks, which the Icelandic scientists have not been able to handle.

Surtsey has thus, in many ways, become an international research centre. Alongside the Icelandic scientists in the field of biology, a team of entomologists from Sweden and a team of marine biologists from Denmark, one limnologist and a microbiologist from Germany are taking part in the research work. Algologists and a geneticist from France are also participating, while both British and American scientists have been engaged in various fields of geology, geochemistry, geophysics as well as biology on the island. The unusually good opportunity for research has enabled many scientists to investigate special subjects which Surtsey has provided. On the island was a barren territory, completely devoid of life, like a part of a dead moon. It was not surprising that astronauts became interested in a visit to the island. There it was possible to study the first signs of life, to ascertain what forms of life were the most likely to be carried by men, and which living organisms would be able to settle on the completely sterile lava and pumice dust. The results of the research on Surtsey might even give some clues as to what precautions should be taken to prevent the contamination of other planets.

It might even be possible to compare Surtsey with some area in which life has been destroyed: for example, regions which have been affected by nuclear action. On Surtsey it would be possible to follow in stages how life would re-inhabit and colonise such areas.

In the beginning, the volcanologists were most interested in studying the constructive forces that made the island. Later, the scientific emphasis shifted from geology to biology. The exobiologist and the microbiologist were most eager to study the thermal sites and other extreme environments. They have been followed by scientists of many sub-disciplines of ecology.

REFERENCES

YOUNG, J. I., *The prose Edda of Snorri Sturluson: Tales from Norse mythology*, Bowes and Bowes, London, 131 (1954)

HERMANNSSON, S., The Surtsey Research Society, Introductions in the *Proceedings* (1967) and *Progress Reports* of the Surtsey Research Society 1 (1965); 2 (1966); 3 (1967); 4 (1968); 5 (1970) and 6 (1972)

FRIDRIKSSON, S., 'Life and its development on the volcanic island, Surtsey', *Surtsey Research Conference, Proceedings*, Reykjavik, 7–19 (1967)

2

GEOLOGICAL NOTES

In the beginning
not anything existed
there was no sand nor sea
nor cooling waves.
Völuspá

In the beginning—there was no sand—there was no island. For a long time there had been no volcanic activities in the ocean south of Iceland. Nobody expected an eruption out at sea, and there was no warning or a prelude to this incident that could have been a definite indication of an eruption.

One may, however, say that volcanic activity is not an unusual phenomenon in Iceland. There is in fact, on the average, an eruption every fifth year. Thus there have been over 200 eruptions during the last 1100 years, which span the historic period of Iceland. Ten to fifteen thousand years have elapsed since Iceland was relieved of the glacial dome covering the country during the last glaciation, and during this post-glacial period at least 150 volcanoes have been active.

This, however, is not an exact figure, as it is very difficult to be precise in evaluating what is one crater. A 20 or 30 km long fissure might suddenly crack open, emitting lava from various centres, and build up a row of up to 100 craters during a single eruption, as in the Laki crater row, formed in 1783 and from which lava has flooded over an area of 565 sq. km. Some of these craters might later unite with the progress of the volcanic activity or during a later eruption in the same fissure. New craters may develop, covering the earlier formations and making it disputable whether one should count one or more craters. A good example is the most famous volcano in Iceland, Mt Hekla, which has been formed on a fissure running south-west to north-east and has during numerous eruptions in post-glacial time built up a 10 km long and a 1491 m high mountain ridge.

During the last ice-age, i.e. in the Pleistocene epoch, most of the volcanoes never emerged above the glacial dome and the movement of ice has obscured many of the volcanic centres formed during that period. The volcanic activity that took place under the glacier did not produce the usual form of lava. The emerging magma undergoes a rapid cooling when it reaches the water from the melted ice. It then splits up into small particles of ash, pops up into pumice or rolls out in lava tongues and intrusions that crack up when cooled and solidify rapidly into pillars and angular fragments of lava. All these eruption products, which are called tephra, later consolidate, the mass of basaltic glass cements together and turns into the brownish vitreous breccia called palagonite.

The eruptions that took place under the 1000 m thick glacier of the ice-age were as today either from central vents or along fissures. Subglacial eruptions from the latter type built up elongated and sometimes non-continuous tuff ridges. Those from a single crater piled up a cone which developed into steep-sided mountains capped with layers of lava.

When such an eruption starts under a glacier, the ice is in the beginning melted above the vent and a lake is formed within the ice. As the eruption progresses, pillow lava and cinder are piled up within the lake, which is dammed up by the ice wall on all sides. The enveloping ice also hinders the spreading of the tephra, which is stacked up and may eventually reach above the water surface or even above the glacial dome.

When the extruding magma no longer comes into contact with the cooling water, viscous lava starts flowing and consolidating into a flat or convex shield on top of the tuff cone. After the retreat of the glacier the mountain stacks are left protruding high above the plateau, which was previously the old foundation of the glacier. Such mountains now characterise the central part of Iceland and are known as table-mountains.

During interglacial periods in this median region of Iceland the volcanic activity, which probably continued on the same scale as when covered with ice, did not pile up into tuff stacks, but produced lava flows forming a flat volcanic cone or shield volcanoes. Thus there is a great difference in the topography of volcanic areas, depending on the condition during eruptions, whether subglacial or aerial.

On both the east and the west side of this median zone, which lies as a belt across the country, there are regions which are geologically older and different, in so far as the bedrock is mainly built up of plateau basalts deriving from so-called central volcanoes active before the ice-age or in the Tertiary period. In this area are to be found the oldest rocks of Iceland, which are, however, only 20 million years of age. Thus Iceland is geologically speaking a very young country.

This juvenility is an outstanding feature of the landscape that shows the barren volcanoes, the open lava fissures and tectonic faults, and the many rough lava flows estimated to be one third of those recorded on earth for the last five hundred years. These lava flows cover approximately one ninth of the total area of Iceland.

Glaciers cover 11 800 sq. km or 11.5% of the area. These are of various types, ranging from mere snow-caps on mountain peaks to extensive plateau ice-domes with glacier tongues moving down to the lowland. From the glaciers run muddy rivers constantly changing course over moraines, glacial deposits, alluvial sands and vast areas of black basaltic pumice. Tremendous floods often occur in these glacial rivers, when volcanic activities take place under the glacier or when ice-dammed lakes are suddenly emptied. The glaciers with their rivers and floods and the abrasive activities of the Atlantic waves have produced a smooth black sandy coast stretching all the way along the south shore of Iceland. This smooth sand is in contrast to the eroded peaks of palagonite rock which stick up here and there by the sea side and to the white glaciers which in places even run all the way down to the ocean.

Farther inland the contours are sometimes very rough, and rocks and mountain cliffs sculptured by the eroding forces of wind, water and ice are clearly exposed as the vegetation cover is at its minimum. There are hardly any woods, which in most other countries give the well-known softness to the scenery. In Iceland the wind has carried away a good deal of the former inland vegetation cover, and there has been an increased erosion since man settled in Iceland and brought in his domestic animals. Some of the soil has been blown away, leaving the barren bedrock or the gaps in the vegetation cover with its exposed soil profiles.

The air is clear, and there is a bright display of colours that further accentuate the crudeness of the landscape and stress the fact that Iceland is a young country still in the making.

Probably the colours are the brightest and show the greatest variety of display in the areas of rhyolite rocks, which are of higher silicon content than the basalt. The colours from these rocks can vary from bright yellow, pink, red and pitch-black to the glassy version called obsidian. In the distance the rhyolitic outcrops in the basalt mountains are like sunny spots that shine even on a rainy day, and the obsidian lava flows, black as coal, have an unrealistic glassy appearance.

In the rhyolitic areas hot mud-pits, fumaroles or solfataras are common phenomena, lending a creative effect to the landscape. Such steaming areas of high temperature are closely connected with volcanic activities, and a volcanic eruption might begin with an increased spouting and splashing of a solfatara area like the eruption of Askja in 1961, or an eruption will finally end in a formation of fumaroles that will continue to eject steam for a long time after lava has ceased to flow. There are many such high temperature areas in Iceland. The heat and high acidity have dissolved the rock into a mass of plastic-clay or paste, which simmers in large basins or small pots, giving off a sulphurous smell and a hissing sound as it bubbles and boils.

In these steaming areas colours are scattered over the surface as on a painter's palette. These high temperature areas are mostly confined to the volcanically active zone of Iceland. In addition, several hundred hot water springs are spread all over the country. In contrast to the fumaroles, the hot water springs are low temperature areas. Some of them are only lukewarm, while others spout boiling hot water. The most famous spouting hot spring in Iceland is Geysir in Haukadalur, which has given its name to all spouting hot springs on earth. During its most powerful ejections it can spout a water column up to 60 m high. The most productive hot spring, however, is the spring in Deildartunga which has the world record in hot water flow and produces 250 litres of boiling water per second.

Most of these hot water springs are used throughout the country for swimming-pools and greenhouses or for the heating of Icelandic homes, as is the case in the capital Reykjavik, which got its name, meaning smoky bay, from the steaming springs that have now been utilised for the benefit of the city. The water in these springs is mostly alkaline with a sulphurous smell, but on the south-western peninsula, Reykjanes, there are salt water springs into which ocean water must seep at lower levels. It is also known that this heat and hot water emission is not confined to the dryland alone. Hot water flows out at the shores and has even been recorded on the ocean floor off the coast of Iceland. Thus it is obvious that the volcanic activities extend across the country and beyond it both towards the north and the south.

REFERENCES

KJARTANSSON, G., 'A comparison of tablemountains in Iceland and the volcanic island of Surtsey off the south coast of Iceland', *Náttúrufr.*, **36**, 1–34 (1966)

KJARTANSSON, G., 'Volcanic forms at the sea bottom', *Iceland and mid-ocean ridges, Symposium, Proceedings* (Edited by S. Björnsson), *Societas Scientiarum Islandica, Rit,* **37**, 53–64 (1967)

BÁRDARSON, H., *Ice and Fire,* Reykjavik, 171 (1971)

THORARINSSON, S., Iceland, *Geography of Norden,* 10, J. W. Cappelens Forlag, Oslo (1960)

3

THE MID-ATLANTIC RIDGE

Loki had three children by the giantess in Giantland called Angrboda (Boder-of-sorrow), the first was the wolf Fenrir, the second Jörmungandur—that is the Midgard Serpent—and the third Hel

. . . . And when they came to him [All-father], he flung the serpent into the deep sea which surrounds the whole world, and it grew so large that it now lies in the middle of the ocean round the earth, biting its own tail. . . .

[and at the end] the sea will lash against the land because the Midgard Serpent is writhing in giant fury trying to come ashore.

The Deluding of Gylfi

The median zone of Iceland, which has been volcanically active in the Quaternary period since about three million years ago, is a belt that runs across the centre of the country from south-west to north-east, covering about 40% of the total area of Iceland. This belt is actually a part of the Mid-Atlantic Ridge that runs through the middle of the floor of the Atlantic Ocean north from Jan Mayen in the Arctic across Iceland through the Azores and Tristan da Cunha south to Bouvet Island in the Antarctic, and is probably a part of a much larger system of ridges and rifts which may be contours of huge masses of the earth's crust separated by fractures. It is believed that these masses may be drifting about, and that over periods of millions of years whole continents may have drifted tens or hundreds of miles. Iceland is one of the places where such a movement can possibly be measured.

A number of eruptions have occurred along this Atlantic Ridge in latter years, such as those of the Icelandic volcanoes Hekla in 1946 and Askja in 1961. An eruption occurred on the island of Fayal in the Azores in 1957 and in Tristan da Cunha in 1961, Surtsey in 1963, on Jan Mayen in 1970, and again near Hekla in 1970. And whenever the Midgard Serpent wriggles, action may be expected in one of its humps.

13

These islands are all points on the ridge system that appear above the ocean, but volcanic activities may also take place anywhere along this line and be unobserved, as the great ocean depths hinder the emersion of the volcanic activities. Only at the high level of the ridges and on the top of the peaks, such as on the above-mentioned islands, are the volcanic activities observable.

There may be many controversial problems concerning this rift structure, theories of continental drifts and spreading of the ocean floor, but it is reasonable to assume that on the islands the geological features are similar to those on the submarine part of the ridge. Although investigations are now being carried out on this submarine part of the ridge, many of the similar phenomena are easier to observe in Iceland.

Thus the volcanic activities which took place subglacially in Iceland during the ice-age may in many ways be paralleled with any submarine volcanic activity.

In Iceland the volcanic ridges run parallel to the fissures across the island, and in a similar way it is known that on the ocean floor there are chains of mountains with peaks reaching a height of 3000 m and separated by deep submarine valleys. These are mere continuations of the geological formations that are easily accessible on the Icelandic dryland. As previously stated, the hot water areas exist both on land and on the ocean floor, and occasionally an eruption takes place from the continental shelf surrounding Iceland.

SUBMARINE ERUPTIONS OFF THE COASTS OF ICELAND

By the flat sandy shore off the southern coast of Iceland a group of islands rise high above the surface of the sea. These are the Westman Islands (Vestmannaeyjar), a group of islands and skerries of which Surtsey is the newest member. All these islands are of volcanic origin and have presumably either been created under ice or in the ocean by the end of or after the last glacial period. Actually, some of the inland mountain stacks on the southern mainland, which are now surrounded by sand, may similarly have been formed by submarine volcanism by the end of the ice-age, at which time the ocean level was up to 60 km farther inland. Later there has been an uplift of the country, and at the same time alluvial deposits from glaciers and rivers as well as lava flows have extended the shoreline to the present level.

The formation of these mountain stacks and islands is all prehistoric, and although it is stated in the *Icelandic Book of Settlement*, which was written in the twelfth century, that the first man to settle in the Westman Islands had built his farm 'where now is burned lava', it has been proven by dating the ash layers chronologically, as well as the lava field formed by the stately volcano Helgafell (Holy Mountain) on the main island, that no previous volcanic activities have taken place on that island in historic time. On the other hand, it is known from written sources that submarine eruptions have occurred farther west off the shore of the Reykjanes peninsula, where it is possible to follow a submarine ridge way out into the Atlantic. Volcanic activities on this ridge have probably taken place more frequently than has been recorded, but during the thirteenth century eruptions seem to have been particularly frequent.

It is stated that in the year 1211 a number of farms were ruined by an earthquake that struck the southern part of the country. 'Then Sörli Kolsson discovered the new Fire Islands (Eldeyjar); the others that had previously always been there had disappeared.' It must thus have been recognised that the previous islands had also been of volcanic origin and may have been formed sometime during the period that had elapsed since the start of the settlement of Iceland in 874. In 1226 an eruption recurred off the coast of Reykjanes with ash-fall so thick that day was dark at noon, and the following winter was, due to the pumice, named the sandy winter. Eruptions are recorded in annals from 1231, 1238 and 1246, when the sun turned crimson and earthquakes were frequent. It is further stated that in 1285 some mystical Thunder Islands (Duneyjar) had been discovered west of Iceland, but whether this was in connection with volcanic activities is not known.

These frequent eruptions out in the ocean during the thirteenth century were quoted in European literature, and many medieval scholars wrote about the natural wonders of Iceland, where both the ocean and the mountains were on fire.

Then came a quiet period lasting until the fifteenth century. At that time it was quoted in the annals for the year 1422 that an eruption had started in the ocean south-west of Reykjanes, and—quoting the annal—'an island emerged which ever after can be seen by those that pass by'. In 1583 an eruption once more took place out in the ocean, being observed from a ship, and in 1783 an eruption started in the ocean seven miles west of Reykjanes, producing an island which emitted ashes and pumice and made sailing treacherous. The island was named Nýey (The New Island) and was the following spring to be formally dedicated to the Danish king to prevent other nationalities from claiming it. This, however, never came to pass, as before the official ceremony could take place the island had completely vanished. In 1830 and 1879 there again occurred submarine eruptions in the same area, but islands were apparently not formed. During the former volcanic activities there were frequent earthquakes that shook down the outermost skerry, a pillar named Geirfuglasker (Great Auk Skerry). And as it tumbled down it became quite disastrous for the bird *Alca impennis*, which thereby lost its main breeding-ground. Shortly afterwards this rare bird completely disappeared, and it is now extinct.

A description is also to be found of an eruption in the ocean north of Iceland, but although several submarine eruptions have occurred there, only three times have islands been formed and none of them has remained for any length of time.

Less volcanic activities seem to have taken place in the Westman Islands area than along the westernmost side of the ridge. In 1896 fires were seen from land somewhere in the ocean south of the islands, but this was not observed at closer range.

As previously stated, however, all the Westman Islands are of volcanic origin. They are a group of 14 islands, excluding Surtsey, and 30 skerries and solitary rocks which are made of palagonite with fragments of lava flows. The largest island is Heimaey (Home Island), which has been estimated to be at least five or even six thousand years old. There were probably originally two islands that became united by a lava flow produced by an eruption, which also built up the volcanic cone Helgafell with a circular lava crater at the summit. This is the highest mountain in this group of islands. Later, an isthmus of boulders has in addition united the third island with the previous group, forming the 16 sq. km large Heimaey, which is the only island occupied by man. On the island there is a village which in 1963 had 5000 inhabitants, a good harbour and an airport. Most of the inhabitants are engaged in fishing, for the fishing grounds around the islands are particularly prolific. However, man is not the only one seeking food in the rich fishing waters. The area teems with sea-birds, which at the same time add to the fertility of the soil of these islands.

The volcanic cone on Heimaey had clearly shown the volcanic origin of that island. This was further stressed during the eruption in 1973. On many of the outer islands are also to be found remnants of craters, but it is not precisely known when they have erupted.

THE PRELUDE

A small trembling of the earth in Iceland is not particularly an indication of any eruption. Thus nobody connected the slight tremor, which was recorded on the seismograph in Reykjavik during the first week of November 1963, with the events that were later to take place. It was not known either where the centre of origin of this earthquake might have been, nor had anyone paid any attention to the slight rise in temperature of the ocean south of Geirfuglasker, which was the southernmost skerry of the

Westman Islands and a synonym of the pillar that disappeared west of Reykjanes. This slight rise in temperature had been recorded by a fishing-boat on 13 November. In a small area the ocean was found to be two degrees centigrade above the usual, but only later was this to be connected with volcanic activities. Possibly, already at that time there had been some emissions of hot water, or some magma had started to pile up on the ocean floor. Volcanic activity on land sometimes begins with an increased spouting up of a hot spring, but a submarine eruption may need some time to build up enough pressure to reach through the overlying mass of water. Although some movements had started at the bottom, everything was still calm and quiet on the surface.

A few boats were fishing south of Geirfuglasker. Some were sailing with their day's catch towards Peace Harbour of Heimaey town. The various sea-birds had also been occupied with their usual search for food in the area. The stately gannet (*Sula bassana*) with its wide wingspan was diving straight down into the deep from high above. The puffin (*Fratercula arctica*) was ducking into the sea from the surface and lining up a row of minnows in the high, thin and striped, orange beak. Possibly these birds and various members of the unusually rich fauna of these waters had sensed something unusual in their marine habitat as the darkness of the November night descended.

REFERENCES

EINARSSON, TH., *The Eruption in Surtsey in Words and Pictures*, Heimskringla, Reykjavik, 23 (1966)
Annales Islandici 1400–1800, Félagsprentsmiðjan, Reykjavik.
Icelandic book of settlement
Lögmannsannáll
Páls saga biskups
THORARINSSON, S., *Surtsey, the new island in the North Atlantic*, Almenna Bókafélagid, Reykjavik, 63 (1964)

4

THE
ERUPTION
STARTS

The Midgard Serpent will blow so much poison that the whole sky and sea
will be spattered with it. . . .

In this din the sky will be rent asunder and the sons of Muspell ride forth from
it. Surtur will ride first and with him fire blazing both before and behind.
The Deluding of Gylfi

In the early morning of 14 November 1963 the seamen of the fishing-boat
Isleifur II from the Westman Islands had been paying out their line on the
bank south-west of Geirfuglasker. When this was completed at 6.30, they
went down into the forecastle for a hot cup of coffee. Shortly after someone
sniffed a sulphurous smell in the air. This time the cook was not to be
blamed, neither was the exhaust from the engine. They searched for the
reason, but it was still dark and they could find no plausible explanation.
Suddenly the surface of the ocean became unusually rough, and as they
sailed on, dawn began to break. The cook who was on watch then suddenly
observed at some distance astern a cloud of black smoke rising up from the
surface of the sea. This was not a burning boat, signal at sea or oil on fire. No
ship had been so close. Although this was a unique event, the skipper finally
reasoned after seeing in his binoculars black tephra rising in the clouds, that
this could be nothing less than an eruption of a submarine volcano. He
consequently picked up the transmitter and reported the unusual event to
the astonished operator at the coastal radio station in the Westman Islands.
Out of curiosity the skipper sailed his boat so close to the scene that there was
only half a nautical mile between his boat and the rising fumes. Fearing the
increased roughness of the sea and an extension of the activity, the skipper

Figure 4.1. (Above) The first day of the
eruption: a new island is being formed.
(Below) The lava shield in formation.
Vapours arise from the shore as the glowing
lava pours into the ocean

thought it wiser to keep at a safe distance from the column of smoke that was steadily rising higher in the air. And now, in addition, showers of ash and cinder were being thrust up and bombs were flying in all directions, accompanied by lightning flashes. The engineer measured the temperature at the surface and found it 2 °C above the usual. The position of the activities was found to be at 63° 18'N and 20° 36.5'W or 5.5 km south-west of Geirfuglasker. At 3 p.m. two original craters had joined and the jets of tephra were becoming more conspicuous. A cinder cone was gradually being built up from the floor of the 120 m deep ocean. On the morning of 15 November an island was born, as the top of the cinder cone had emerged above the surface. The pile of pumice insulated the emission of heat, and the surface temperature of the ocean around the island returned to normal. The column of clouds, however, rose still higher during the day until it reached a height of 9 km.

During my flight over the eruption site that day it was noticeable that on the windward side the ocean had a brownish-green colour extending only 50 m from the island, whereas on the leeward side the surface was under a constant shower of ash, pumice and bombs a few hundred metres out. The brown pumice was floating on the surface and was gradually being carried away by the ocean currents (Figure 4.1 and Plate 1).

On the third day the cinder cone had reached a height of 40 m. The crater, however, was still split open, and during rhythmical explosions the water was either thrust out or flooded back into the vent. The wind and waves of the North Atlantic constantly washed around the new reef as though they wished to eject this intruder from their waters. These two natural elements, air and water, fought however a hopeless battle against their counterparts, earth and fire, which gradually piled up the cinder cone to an ever increasing height. On 20 November it had reached a height of 70 m, and by February the following year it was 174 m above sea-level.

During the winter storms the island thus fought a hard battle for its survival. Repeatedly the ocean waves entered the crater and broke down high cinder hills and pumice ridges which had been built up during calmer weather, and with the wind shifting from one side to the other, the entrance in the wall through which the water could stream into the crater likewise changed position. And as the water came into contact with the flowing magma deep in the shaft of the vent an explosion took place. During such explosions no sound was heard, but a mass of black tephra rushed up and often fanned out into numerous plume-like jets, which from a distance looked like a bundle or a puff of black feathers turning greyish-brown as they advanced into the air. There the vapour was skimmed from the ash particles like the grey fringe of a feather that flew off and joined thousands of others to form the downy quilt of a cloud hovering above the crater. Some

Figure 4.2. (Above) A view of the craters formed during the eruption which started on 19 August 1966. (Below) The ropy lava with the relatively smooth surface of the pahoe-hoe or hellu lava type

Figure 4.3. One of the fumaroles produced during the New Year's eruption

of these protuberances reached a height of several hundred metres and were thrust up at a speed of 100 m per second; swayed by the wind they often curved out from the island, discharging the tephra that fell over the edges of the crater or into the sea. Frequently a bomb drove the foremost tip of the feather up into the air and then fell into the ocean, forming a spout of sizzling water.

During this phase of the eruption the ocean was in constant contact with the magma, and a cauliflower column of vapour clouds reached high up in the air, while the ash fell downwind from the island like a black curtain with vertical stripes of intense or light ash, depending on the amount of ash produced by the pulsating explosions. Sometimes the ash particles became coated with vapour or ice, which fell down as a shower of rain or hail. Sometimes only a mixture of sea salt and ash fell down, vapour being released into the cloud. At other times a whirlwind was seen spinning down from the column of vapour clouds agitating the water below, or with the lower end curving inwards towards the island as a result of the centric draught following the updrift of air caused by the volcanic activities. Most of the ash particles fell on the island or were carried a few hundred metres downwind. However, during intense activities when the cloud columns even reached

Plate 1. On the morning of 15 November an island was born which later was given the name Surtsey

Plate 2. The lava crater with glowing magma

Plate 3. *Rivulets of red-hot magma oozed out and formed lava with a relatively smooth surface*

Plate 4. *A shield of lava was built up on the south side of the island. The magma ran down to the sea and as it fell into the ocean a fringe of steam was ejected along the shore*

up into the stratosphere, fine dust particles were carried several kilometres or even hundreds of kilometres away. The distant spread of volcanic ash at high altitude was noticed from aeroplanes passing across the Atlantic. Similar ash discharge has since been photographed from satellites: like the 200 mile long ash plume formed in September 1970 during the eruption of the Beerenberg volcano on Jan Mayen Island. This smoke line could be detected as it contrasted sharply with the cold, dark water south of the volcanic island. During south-western winds ash fell in the town of Heimaey causing some nuisance, as at that time fresh water had not been piped to the village from the mainland; the water used by the islanders being mostly rain-water collected from roof tops. Although the eruption looked rather threatening to the neighbourhood it did not however result in any catastrophic effects on life on the Westman Islands.

During the period of the eruption lightning was often seen flashing up the ash-grey column. The ejecta from the eruption was highly electrified, the clouds being positively charged. The potential gradient formed was most intense near the crater. After a black jet had been thrust up, a lightning flash frequently followed 10 to 50 seconds later, neutralising or lowering the positive charge towards the earth.

The active vents sometimes shifted from one side of the crater to the other, and when finally a relatively secure wall was formed only a moderate amount of water seeped through into the vent.

When this occurred there was a change in the activities. Pulsating explosions ceased, and instead a continuous uprush of tephra spouted up, sometimes lit up by splashes of glowing lava fragments and bombs. Actually it was a fountain of lava in the making. But as it was still under the water level it was constantly cooled on the surface, so that only ash and scoria were produced.

This phase of the eruption started towards the end of January 1964. Occasionally during such an uprush the vapour clouds suddenly ceased to rise above the water, probably because the magma surface of the crater was sealed off, with the magma tapped at lower levels flowed through sub-oceanic veins near the seabed.

During one such repose in early February 1964 the most active crater, which had been named Surtur I, completely ceased to erupt. At the same time a new crater started to erupt farther to the west on the island. North of this crater an explosion probably occurred in early February, forming a depression that filled up with water and became a lagoon.

The new centre of activity, named Surtur II, mostly erupted with a continuous uprush of tephra. This crater was very productive in building up the island, as a great amount of material was constantly being ejected and thrown upon the crater walls, which on the west side reached an elevation

(a)

(b)

Figure 4.4. (a) A landing on Surtsey in a rubber dinghy. The satellite island of Syrtlingur is seen erupting in the distance. (b) A view of the scientists' hut. The lagoon in the background partly filled by the New Year's lava

24

of 169 m above the ocean level. Some of the ejecta was in the form of lava fragments or bombs that were even hurled to a height of 2.5 km. By the end of March 1964, Surtsey had grown to a size of 1 sq. km.

THE LAVA FLOW

The eruption from the crater named Surtur II was gradually becoming less explosive until finally on 4 April 1964 the volcanic shaft obtained a water-tight lining of lava and the ocean no longer flooded over the crater wall. When this occurred, the surface of magma in the vent was no more affected by the constant cooling of the water and the floating lava emerged above sea-level. Lava fountains were formed, spouting 50 to 100 m high columns of glowing magma that bubbled and splashed up from a red-hot lake. All around the lake the lava splashes moulded a sort of huge vase, inside which the magma level either rose or fell with variations in the volcanic activity (Plate 2). Sometimes the magma overflowed the rim, and floods of thin magma swept down from the crater over the island, gushing towards the sea with a speed of up to 70 km per hour. When this magma solidified, it formed a relatively smooth surface of lava, which was of the pahoe-hoe or *hellu* lava type as it is called in Icelandic (Figure 4.2). Other streams of magma, which ran more slowly, solidified into lava with a rough surface, forming the aa or *apal* lava type. This new chapter of volcanic activity has by the geologists been called the effusive phase and does not differ markedly from eruptions on land. With every new flow pouring out of the crater a new layer of lava appeared. Thus, gradually a hard shield of lava was formed over the relatively loose tephra of the cone that had been produced during the explosive phase of the eruption.

The hard shell formed on the loose tephra was as though some icing had been smeared on a devil's food cake. The coating of lava gave the island a hard crust, protecting it from the erosive actions of wind and water. And as this effusive phase of the eruption progressed, a dome of lava was gradually being formed. Like wax driblets on an old candlestick, magma constantly streamed over the crater's rim and ran down to the sea, sometimes as red-hot surface rivulets (Plate 3), or more often in closed veins from which the magma oozed out at lower levels or dripped into the sea. And as it flowed with a temperature of 1100 °C and fell as red lava balls into the ocean, steams of vapour were whipped up to form a white fringe around the edge of the island (Plate 4). The rapidly cooled magma formed lava tongues as it ran along the sea shore or broke up into small glassy fragments, which were carried along the shore and deposited on the leeward side, forming a sandy beach in the northern part of the island.

25

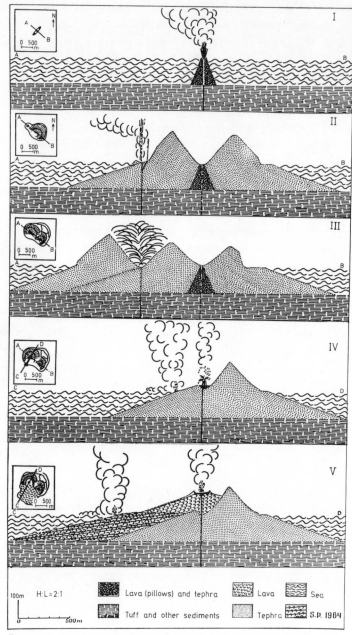

Figure 4.5. A schematic drawing of the upbuilding of the island (Courtesy: S. Thorarinsson)

By the end of April the lava crater had reached a height of 90 m above sea-level, and for some months the surface flow from the magma lake was interrupted, but apparently at the same time it flooded through subterranean and sub-oceanic veins, still further strengthening the island fortress against the ocean waves that constantly pounded it from the south. During the repose of the surface flow, the sea-surge broke the edge of the lava, forming cliffs by the shore, and churned up the broken rocks or rolled and polished them into rounded boulders, which were—like the sand—also carried over to the northern side. When the magma resumed its flow from the crater in early July, the magma lake was 100 m in diameter, and from it the magma poured down the consolidated shield and tumbled off the cliffs into the ocean in golden lava-falls. These activities continued with various intervals until 7 May 1965, by which time the permanence of Surtsey was assured and a solid lava surface of 1.5 sq. km had been formed on the southern side of the island (Plate 5).

On 19 August 1966 a 200 m long fissure opened up across the eastern part of the island through the old Surtur crater, forming a row of small craters from which lava flowed towards the east coast (Plate 6). This fissure broke through the cinder cone on 1 January 1967 and magma started to flow towards the north. It flooded into the lagoon on the north shore, partly filling it and even threatening to destroy the scientists' hut, which had been erected at the foot of the hill on the northern side of the island (Figures 4.3 and 4.4). The lava flow from the northern crater, however, lasted only a few days, whereas south of the cinder cone the activities continued until 5 June 1967, when lava was last seen flowing from Surtsey island (Figure 4.5).

REFERENCES

EINARSSON, TH., 'Studies of temperature, viscosity, density and some types of materials produced in the Surtsey eruption', *Surtsey Res. Progr. Rep.*, **2**, 163–179 (1966)

EINARSSON, TH., *The Eruption in Surtsey in Words and Pictures*, Heimskringla, Reykjavik, 23 (1966)

EINARSSON, TH., 'Der Surtsey Ausbruch', *Naturwiss Rundschau*, **20**, 239–247 (1967)

Nimbus. Earth Resources Observations, Technical Report No. 2, National Aeronautic Space Administration, 69–72 (1971)

The Best of Nimbus, National Aeronautic and Space Administration, 83 (1971)

THORARINSSON, S., 'Surtsey island born of fire', *National Geographic Magazine*, **127**, No. 5 (1965)

THORARINSSON, S., 'The Surtsey eruption. Course of events and the development of Surtsey and other new islands', *Surtsey Res. Progr. Rep.* **2**, 77–87 (1966)

THORARINSSON, S., 'Review of geological and geophysical research connected with the Surtsey eruption', *Surtsey Research Conference Proceedings*, Reykjavik, 20–29 (1967)

THORARINSSON, S., 'The Surtsey Eruption. Course of events during the year 1966', *Surtsey Res. Progr. Rep.*, **3**, 84–92 (1967)

THORARINSSON, S., *Surtsey, the new island in the North Atlantic*, Viking Press, New York (1967)

THORARINSSON, S., 'Island is born' (excerpt from above), *Reader's Digest*, **92**, Feb. 146–153 (1968)

THORARINSSON, S., 'The Surtsey Eruption. Course of events during the year 1967', *Surtsey Res. Progr. Rep.*, **4**, 143–149 (1968)

THORARINSSON, S., EINARSSON, TH., SIGVALDASON, G. and ELISSON, G., 'The submarine eruption off the Westman Islands 1963–1964', *Bulletin Volcanologique*, **27**, 1–11 (1964)

5

THE FORMATION AND DISAPPEARANCE OF ISLETS

The sun will go black, earth sink in the sea, heaven be stripped of its bright stars, smoke rage and fire, leaping the flame, lick heaven itself.

The Deluding of Gylfi

Parallel with the eruption on Surtsey, volcanic activities took place in the area around the main island and acted like side vents to the main craters, starting whenever the activities ceased on Surtsey.

Thus from the ocean floor east of Surtsey some activity took place during the period December 1963 to January 1964. From the splashing surface bombs were thrown up into the air, but an island never emerged.

During May to October 1965 submarine activities started 600 m east of Surtsey. In a similar way as the Surtsey eruption commenced, these activities developed slowly with water-spouts and emissions of pumice that drifted from the eruption sites. Then the explosive phase, so familiar from the Surtsey eruption, started, and during the fifth day an island was born. The following months this island, which was called Syrtlingur (Little Surtur), piled up until it became 70 m high and attained an area of 0.15 sq. km (Plate 7). (See Figures 5.1 and 6.4 for position of islets.)

During Christmas 1965 still another submarine outbreak started 900 m to the south-west of Surtsey. Shortly afterwards an island was formed which the eruptive forces, however, had difficulty in maintaining during the winter storms. The volcanological story was repeated once more with an explosive uprush of cinder, ash and pumice that lasted until August 1966, and with

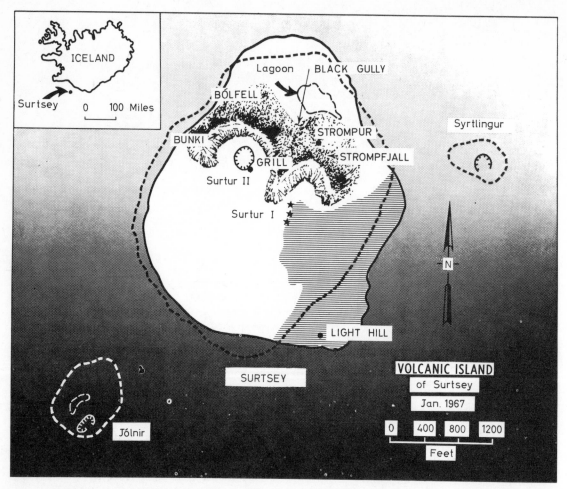

Figure 5.1. A chart showing Surtsey and the two satellite islands Syrtlingur and Jólnir. These islets have now disappeared. The stars indicate the craters formed in August 1966. The broken line shows the shoreline as it appeared on 19 August 1966 compared with that of January 1967 (Courtesy: U.S. Dept. of the Interior: Geological Survey)

Plate 5. An aerial view of Surtsey in eruption. The satellite islands had not yet appeared. The other Westman Islands are in the distance with Heimaey farther away

Plate 6. An erupting crater on the fissure that opened up across the eastern part of the island on 19 August 1966

Plate 7. The plumes of the cloud emitted from the island of Syrtlingur were similar to those formed during the explosive phase of the Surtsey eruption

Plate 8. Sulphurous deposits on the recently formed lava

Plate 9. A boulder rim extends along the shore and gives Surtsey the appearance of an old island

vapour clouds that reached up to a height of 6000 m. This island also attained a height of 70 m and an area of almost 0.3 sq. km.

It received the name of Jólnir, one of many synonyms of the leading Norse God and also referring to the island's birth on Boxing Day (yule), or Christmas island. These two smaller islands were formed, just like the pedestal of Surtsey, by explosive activities that piled up a submarine cinder cone which eventually emerged above the ocean level. From their craters pumice floated along to the shores of Surtsey and the showers of tephra thrown up in the air were often spread by wind over the surface of Surtsey, covering areas of the old tuff cone and lava with a layer of ash and cinder up to several feet in thickness. Viewed from Surtsey, these ash clouds often blackened the sun. The islands were built up of loose tephra. Without a lava crust they could not take the beating of the North Atlantic waves. Thus their survival was never assured, and they have both disappeared—'the earth sank in the sea'. And where there were islands, only shoals remain at a depth of 20 to 40 m below the ocean level (Figure 5.1).

REFERENCES

EINARSSON, TH., *The Eruption in Surtsey in Words and Pictures*, Heimskringla, Reykjavik, 23 (1966)

MALMBERG, S. A., 'Beam transmittance measurements carried out in the waters around Surtsey', *Surtsey Res. Progr. Rep.*, **4**, 195–197 (1968)

SIGVALDASON, G. E., 'Structure and products of subaquatic volcanoes in Iceland', *Surtsey Res. Progr. Rep.*, **4**, 141–143 (1968)

THORARINSSON, S., *Surtsey, the new island in the North Atlantic*, Almenna Bókafélagid, Reykjavik, 63 (1964)

6

LANDSCAPE

They took Ymir and carried him into the middle of Ginnungagap, and made the world from him; from his blood the sea and lakes, from his flesh the earth, from his bones the mountains, rocks and pebbles they made from his teeth and jaws and those bones that were broken.

The Deluding of Gylfi

The small islands markedly affected the surface on Surtsey, although their existence above water was not of great duration. Their fate was the same as that of many islands previously built up along the Icelandic coast by submarine eruptions. Their activities started on a fissure, and from one or more craters the lava oozed out and piled up into pillow lava on the ocean floor, while the hydrostatic pressure prevented the natural degassing of the material. This continued until the opening of the vent moulded by the lava pile had reached closer to the surface. From measurements of the substantial shoals this level seems to be at about a depth of 40 m. Then the hydraulic pressure becomes low enough to allow the dissolved gases of the magma to explode the material into fine tephra. Thus the lava core is not extended any higher, unless the activities are long-lasting and the cinder piles become so advanced and enjoy such calmness of the sea that a watertight lining of a vent might be formed.

In the Westman Islands archipelago extensive volcanism has taken place within an area of 700 sq. km, forming at least 60 submarine craters during the last fifteen thousand years that have never emerged or only formed islands that have later broken down. The islands we see there today have proven more substantial.

When Surtsey obtained its hard lava shield, it was foreseen that it would be one of the long-lasting members of the islands in the archipelago.

The volcanic material formed during the Surtsey eruption is estimated to be about 1.1 cubic km, of which 70% was tephra. Only 9% of this material is above sea-level, and this had formed an area of 2.8 sq. km by the end of the eruption.

THE TEPHRA

The two tephra cones of the craters Surtur I and Surtur II form the major parts of the western and central regions of the island. In these sections there are high ridges and hills of cinder and ash with fragments of scoria, or tuff material which is gradually undergoing palagonitisation.

The fresh basaltic glass sideromelane started to consolidate shortly after the tuff was produced, especially at the thermal fields with temperatures of 60 to 100 °C, and after a few years it was transforming into the dense brown palagonite tuff called *móberg* in Icelandic. During palagonitisation, water enters the particles and iron becomes oxidised, whereas various elements are lost, such as Ca and Na. The ions which are thus liberated may be found in solution on the glass grains and will be available to organisms that may later colonise the tephra.

This tuff material was continuously mixed with ocean water as it was being piled up during the explosive phase of the eruption. When tested for soluble mineral content three years after the start of the eruption, it still had high salt content.

When leachate from the tuffaceous material was compared with sea-water, it was noticed that the former contained a large amount of $CaSO_4$ in excess of that in normal sea-water (Plate 8). These minerals must have precipitated and not leached out of the tuff to the same extent as other components during rainy weather or been released by the palagonitisation. A slight increase, relative to sea-water, was also found in other components, such as Na, K and Mg.

The tephra consists of stratigraphic levels with grains of different texture and size, the particles being sorted out by the variation in the force of explosion as well as the wind direction and velocity during the dispersal of tephra from the vents through the air. Airborne grains, however, are not assorted according to size to the same extent as when they are deposited in the sea-water. More than 90% of particles on the island fall in sizes between 0.05 to 5 mm.

The tephra cones reach a height of 170 m, which is the highest point of the island. On the northern and western sides they slope down to level beach, but

Figure 6.1. (Left) A slope of tephra cone, the western Bunki, showing slumping and the bolder ridge. (Below) An aerial view of the western coast and the slopes of the tephra cone, western Bunki (Photo: S. Magnússon)

towards the south the cones only protrude 50 to 70 m up above the lava shield. As the tephra material is still very loose in texture, it is rapidly eroded by wind and water.

On the western side of the island the waves from south-west and west are constantly undercutting the slope, causing slumps and avalanches from the highest hill. These wave actions have formed a sharply eroded, steep wall that is gradually extending towards the inner edge of the western rim of the Surtur II crater. A further retreat of the edge will begin to lower the high points of the island. Furthermore, rain-water washes and carries away the fine dust of this substrate to lower levels (Figure 6.1). Thus the sides of the cinder cones are lined with vertical furrows formed by mud flows that deposit the silt in dumps at the foot of the hills.

The wind also plays its part in blowing the tephra about, eroding the sides and peaks of the hills and depositing the silt at lower levels.

THE LAVA

The shield consists of many horizontal beds of basaltic lava formed during the last part of the Surtsey eruption. Although of relatively stable material, it has constantly been under the influence of erosive elements both during and after the volcanic activities.

At the end of the eruption the section of the lava shield that was above sea-level covered an area of 1.4 sq. km, which fanned out over the southern part of the island. With every year that passes, the ocean continues cutting down its edges and is rapidly trimming off the fringes shaping the uneven southern border into a smooth coastline.

Annually there has been a 30 m retreat of the southern shoreline. This has resulted in a formation of vertical cliffs that are 5 to 12 m high on the average, but have been found to reach a height of 32 m on the south-western shore (Figure 6.2).

On the south-eastern coast there is less abrasion. The surface of the shield is both that of the smooth and the rough type of lava. The lava from the first outbreak of Surtur II was mostly overlaid with cinder deposited from the eruptions of the small islands Syrtlingur and Jólnir. This lava covers approximately an area of 0.7 sq. km, which is half of the total lava cover of the island, the other half being formed by the flow from the August craters (Figure 6.3). This surface is also gradually being filled up with tephra and sand that drifts from the shores and is blown from the cinder cones, filling up the numerous cracks and crevices of the rough lava surface. Close to the cones the lava has in this way been almost totally covered with sand deposits. The lava beds lying closer to the shore still, however, remain quite bare.

Figure 6.2. Twenty to thirty metre high cliffs have been formed by the cutting of the ocean waves on the south-eastern shore. Big blocks are cut from the lava and rounded into boulders or sometimes thrown up on the cliffs edge (Photo: S. Magnússon)

Figure 6.3. An aerial view of the lava apron showing the two craters Surtur I (right) and Surtur II (left) (Photo: S. Magnússon)

THE COASTAL PLAINS

On the northern side of Surtsey there was originally a lagoon protected to
the north by a low tephra rim and to the south by the cinder cones. It has
gradually been filled up by silt brought down by the mud flows from the
cinder slopes or by sand carried in by sea floods or wind, and also by
the small flow of lava formed by the eruption in January 1967. Most of the
material forming the coastal plain, however, originates from the lava beds
of the southern coast. The lava fragments which are constantly being cut
down from the edge of the lava shield are of various sizes and are rapidly
being abraded into sand grains, pebbles and rounded boulders up to several
cubic metres in size. Most of this material is swept off the platform and
brought towards lower depths, but some is transported by the breakers
along the coasts to be deposited on the shores on either side of the lava or
brought to the northern ness. During the flow of lava in 1966 and 1967
the total area of the island increased, but the abrasion was also great and the
ness was thus rapidly built up. A spit advanced 80 m out, formed by coarse
sand and pebbles; and as it curved towards east it formed and closed off a new
lagoon between two barriers, changing the structure of the coast from the
previous circular or almost rectangular form with rounded corners and gave
it a pear-shaped configuration which is orientated in a north–south direction
(Figure 6.4).

This shaping-up of the island is caused by the predominant waves
generated by low pressure areas moving from the south-west. Boulder
rims run along the shores 4 to 5 m above sea-level, extending from the lava
edges and encircling the ness (Plate 9). These boulders are well rounded
0.5 to 1.5 m in diameter, forming terraces with sand, gravel and cobbles. In
severe winter storms and high tides most of this coastal plain can be flooded
and a high-water mark is found at the foot of the tephra cones (Figure 6.5).
A great part of the ness is now covered with silt, sand and cobbles, with some
boulder ridges and even some small sand dunes. Both the lagoons have been
filled up by beach material.

THERMAL AREAS

Although it was generally considered that the eruption in Surtsey ended on
5 June 1967 when glowing lava was last seen moving on the island, thermal
activity continued, and when this was written in 1973 there were still high
temperature spots on the island. The general locations of thermal areas were
several times detected by thermal infra-red imagery survey. In addition,
more precise surface temperature measurements were taken. The glowing

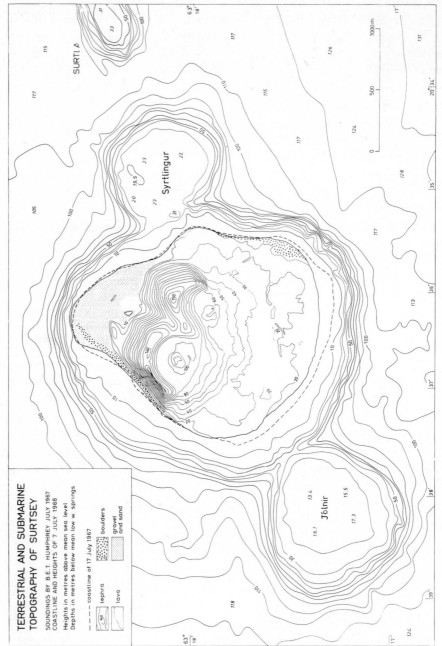

Figure 6.4. Terrestrial and submarine topography of Surtsey (Courtesy: J. O. Norrman)

38

Figure 6.5. A high flood on the northern ness, 8 August 1971 (Photo: S. Magnússon)

magma in the Surtur crater had a temperature of 1130 to 1140 °C. This was measured on two occasions by a 10 m long NiCr/NiAe Pyrotenax thermo-couple. The temperature of magma flowing in a subterranean channel was estimated to be above 1300 °C, but an attempt to obtain a more precise measurement failed, as the electric thermometer, which was protected by an iron cylinder, melted when placed above the lava fissure. In some other veins the flowing magma was at a temperature of only 800 °C, and lower temperatures were measured in secondary fumaroles and in the cooling lava. During the period of three years and seven months which the eruption of Surtsey lasted, it is estimated that the energy generated was enough to raise the temperature of one cubic kilometre of sea by 2 °C. Only a small amount of this energy, however, went into heating sea–water, due to the insulation effect of the tephra, but was released into the atmosphere.

In 1970 an overall survey of surface temperatures was carried out on the island, utilising thermistor-type thermometers for the range up to 120 °C and Rototherm thermocouple probe for the range 100 °C to 550 °C. The thermal area was found to be mostly confined to the location of the 'primary' energy source at the central craters of Surtur I and II with the exception of an isolated spot in the southern part of the lava shield. In this local hot spot

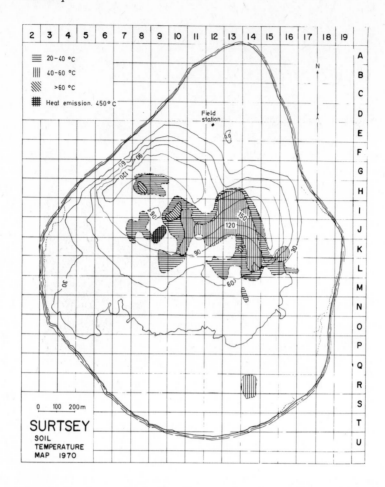

Figure 6.6.
A chart showing the thermal areas on Surtsey in 1970

there may be an emission from a slowly cooling sub-surface lava, that is a secondary source of thermal energy.

In the main thermal area the heat is emitted both through the tephra of Surtur I as well as the lava of Surtur II. In the tephra crater of Surtur I heat is emitted through the interior of the crater bowl. And the thermal area extends over the eastern cinder hill called Chimney Mountain (Strompfjall) and down the slope on its northern side, where there is a fumarole named Chimney (Strompur). The Chimney, made of dark lava, sticks up from the side of the tephra cone and emits boiling steam (see the map Figure 5.1).

In the thermal area of the tephra the temperature at a depth of 20 cm is between 40 and 60 °C. Measurements have been made at lower levels, and it seems that the temperatures in the tephra nowhere exceed 100 °C at a depth of 150 cm.

Where the tephra and the lava merge, the temperatures may be somewhat higher, but out of the fissures running into the lava in all directions from the centre of the crater Surtur I steam is emitted with temperatures from 60 to 220 °C. The steam issuing from these fissures and fumaroles or up through the small lava craters is generally at a temperature of 100 °C, but farther out in the lava, where it seems to contain less vapour, 220 °C has been measured.

This thermal area extends between the two Surtur craters, but in the western crater, Surtur II, it is more confined to the lava and extends nowhere more than a few tens of metres out from the edge of the lava into the tephra. In the Surtur II crater the heat is emitted as 100 °C hot steam, up through numerous fissures and cracks, and in a spot on the north-western side of the crater there is an emission of dry hot air with a maximum temperature of 460 °C. This hot air ascends from a fissure with a hissing sound. At the southern edge of this crater there is another high temperature centre called 'The Grill', where there is an upflow of 200 °C hot air that in places is blown out through openings in the lava with a whistling sound. These thermal areas have been registered on an aerial photograph, and on the chart (Figure 6.6) isothermal lines have been drawn, mainly showing the areas with a temperature difference of 30 °C, as well as the hot spots. Outside the thermal areas the temperature at a depth of 20 cm is almost everywhere between 9 and 14 °C.

It is obvious that the geothermal temperature is mostly confined to the shaft of the two large explosive craters. Where the heat is emitted through the tephra, it is cooled down to 100 °C or less by the moisture that this substrate contains, but in the lava it finds easier outlets via cracks and fumaroles through which it is emitted by hot and dry air.

It has been suggested that the slowly cooling pillow-lava which formed the socle of Surtsey during the first phase of the volcanic activity may be generating this heat, and that the heat seeks an outlet through the upper edge of the slanting lava-shield which is like a tilting lid on a hot pot. It is, however, more likely that the thermal source is of primary origin and that the heat finds its way directly from the magma through the crater shaft, and that this thermal emission is a remnant of the same activity that caused the flow of the magma, like hot springs which often develop after the cessation of a volcanic eruption.

REFERENCES

FRIEDMAN, J. D. and WILLIAMS, S. jr., 'Comparison of 1968 infrared imagery of Surtsey', *Surtsey Res. Progr. Rep.*, **5**, 90–95 (1970)

JAKOBSSON, S., 'The geology and petrography of the Westman Islands, A preliminary report', *Surtsey Res. Progr. Rep.*, **4**, 113–129 (1968)

JAKOBSSON, S., 'The consolidation and palagonitisation of the tephra of the Surtsey volcanic island, Iceland, A preliminary report', *Surtsey Res. Progr. Rep.*, **6**, 121–129 (1972)

JÓHANNESSON, A., 'Report on geothermal observations on the island of Surtsey', *Surtsey Res. Progr. Rep.*, **6**, 129–137 (1972)

KJARTANSSON, G., 'A contribution to the morphology of Surtsey', *Surtsey Res. Progr. Rep.*, **2**, 125–129 (1966)

MAGNÚSSON, S., SVEINBJÖRNSSON, B. and FRIDRIKSSON, S., 'Substrate temperature measurements and location of thermal areas on Surtsey, summer 1970', *Surtsey Res. Progr. Rep.*, **6**, 82–85 (1972)

NORRMAN, J. O., 'Shore and offshore morphology of Surtsey, Report on preliminary studies in 1967', *Surtsey Res. Progr. Rep.*, **4**, 131–139 (1968)

NORRMAN, J. O., 'Kustmorphologiska studier på Surtsey', *Svensk Naturvetenskap*, Stockholm (1969)

NORRMAN, J. O., 'Trends in postvolcanic development of Surtsey island, Progress report on geomorphological activities in 1968', *Surtsey Res. Progr. Rep.*, **5**, 95–113 (1970)

NORRMAN, J. O., 'Coastal development of Surtsey island, 1968–1969 ' *Surtsey Res. Progr. Rep.*, **6**, 137–145 (1972)

NORRMAN, J. O., 'Coastal changes in Surtsey island, 1969–1970,' *Surtsey Res. Progr. Rep.*, **6**, 145–150 (1972)

RIST, S., 'Echographic soundings around Surtsey', *Surtsey Res. Progr. Rep.*, **3**, 82–84 (1967)

SHERIDAN, M. F., 'Textural analysis of Surtsey tephra, A preliminary report', *Surtsey Res. Progr. Rep.*, **6**, 150–152 (1972)

SIGVALDASON, G. E. and FRIDRIKSSON, S., 'Water soluble leachate of volcanic ash from Surtsey', *Surtsey Res. Progr. Rep.*, **4**, 163–164 (1968)

THORARINSSON, S., 'The geomorphology of Surtsey', *Surtsey Research Conference, Proceedings*, Reykjavik, 54–58 (1967)

WILLIAMS, R. S., FRIEDMAN, J. D., THORARINSSON, TH., SIGURGEIRSSON, TH. and PÁLMASON, G., 'Analysis of 2966 infrared imagery of Surtsey', *Surtsey Res. Progr. Rep.*, **4**, 173–177 (1968)

7

CLIMATE

Where does the wind come from? It is so strong that it stirs up great seas and fans fire into flame, yet, strong as it is, it can never be seen, so marvellously is it made.

The Deluding of Gylfi

Just as the contrasts of ice and fire characterise the Icelandic landscape, so is the Icelandic climate governed by constant alternation in invasions of either warm air from the Atlantic or cold air sweeping over the country from the Arctic.

Many of the depressions so commonly formed in the western part of the Atlantic move north-eastward and hit the south-west coast of Iceland. As one cyclone follows another and moves across the country, it may carry a warm flow of air causing rain in summer and thaws in winter, and as it passes north winds start blowing, bringing polar air with cool and bright weather in the Westman Islands region in the summer or even snow and blizzards in the winter.

The climate of the Westman Island archipelago is highly oceanic and relatively warm and moist in comparison with the average climate of the mainland. With mild winters and much precipitation, the mean annual temperature is the third highest in Iceland, showing a maximum of 5.7 °C, and only at six other stations in Iceland have annual mean precipitation recordings been higher, the maximum being at Vík in Mýrdal: 2256 mm. South winds are most frequent on the southern coast of Iceland and gales are common. As a matter of fact, the highest wind speed ever measured in

Table 7.1. Mean precipitations and temperatures at Stórhöfdi, Westman Islands; Vík in Mýrdal; and Grímsey, 1901–1930–1960

Meteorological stations	Jan.	Feb.	Mar.	Apr.	May	June	July	Aug.	Sept.	Oct.	Nov.	Dec.	The whole year
						Mean temperatures in °C							
Westman Islands (Stórhöfdi)													
1901–1930	1.1	1.3	1.6	3.0	5.7	8.5	10.2	9.6	7.5	4.8	2.4	1.4	4.8
1931–1960	1.4	1.6	2.7	3.7	6.2	8.5	10.3	10.2	8.4	5.6	3.8	2.5	5.4
Vík in Mýrdal													
1901–1930	0.9	1.2	1.5	3.1	6.2	9.3	11.0	10.5	8.0	4.9	2.3	1.3	5.0
1931–1960	1.2	1.2	2.6	3.9	6.9	9.5	11.3	11.0	9.0	5.6	3.7	2.3	5.7
Grímsey													
1901–1930	−1.8	−1.9	−2.0	−0.8	2.2	5.7	7.7	6.8	5.5	2.6	0.2	−0.9	2.0
1931–1960	−0.5	−1.1	−0.4	0.2	3.4	6.3	8.1	8.3	6.7	3.9	1.9	0.3	3.1
						Precipitation in mm							
Westman Islands (Stórhöfdi)													
1921–1930	160	147	197	99	84	72	90	89	125	93	129	160	1373
1931–1960	138	104	109	97	81	81	84	108	132	166	141	156	1397
Vík in Mýrdal													
1931–1960	182	159	164	171	143	167	169	188	237	238	212	226	2256
Grímsey 1951–1962													662

Iceland, 108 knots or 56 metres per second, occurred in the Westman Islands in October 1963.

Meteorological data have been recorded on Heimaey (Home Island) since 1872. The weather reporting station is located on Stórhöfdi at the southern extremity of the island. There fewer days of frost are recorded than on the mainland, the temperature fluctuations are fairly small and there are by far the most numerous days with fog for the whole of Iceland. The more detailed climatic records are shown in Table 7.1.

In general, climatic conditions in Surtsey do not markedly deviate from

Table 7.2. Mean air temperatures at Surtsey measured in °C

	1967	*1968*
April	3.1	4.1
May	6.0	6.2
June	8.3	8.5
July	9.8	11.2
August	10·3	10.7
September	9.1	9.7

those of Stórhöfdi. Climatic observations on Surtsey started in 1967 when a station was established at the scientists' hut on the western part of the island, north of Bólfell cone. The station has been operating only through the summer months.

When observations are compared with those of Stórhöfdi, it can be seen that the mean temperatures at Surtsey are somewhat higher, or *c.* 1 °C. The mean air temperatures at Surtsey have been found to be as shown in Table 7.2.

The air temperatures on Surtsey have a small daily amplitude due to the proximity of the sea. This is 3 to 4 °C on a sunny day and 1 to 2 °C on overcast days. The soil temperatures have been recorded at depths of 5 cm and 20 cm. In July the mean temperature of the soil is considerably higher than that of the air. The mean temperature at a depth of 5 cm is 14.2 °C and 12.7 °C at 20 cm. The corresponding figures at Reykjavik are 11.2 °C and 9.9 °C.

The soil temperatures recorded show a much higher daily amplitude than the air, a 10 to 12 °C difference being typical in July on a sunny day at 5 cm depth and 2.5 to 3.0 °C at 20 cm depth. The corresponding figures for a cloudy day are 4 °C and 1 °C.

The precipitation on Surtsey is somewhat less than at Stórhöfdi. The records so far obtained show values ranging from 60 to 80% of the corresponding records from Stórhöfdi.

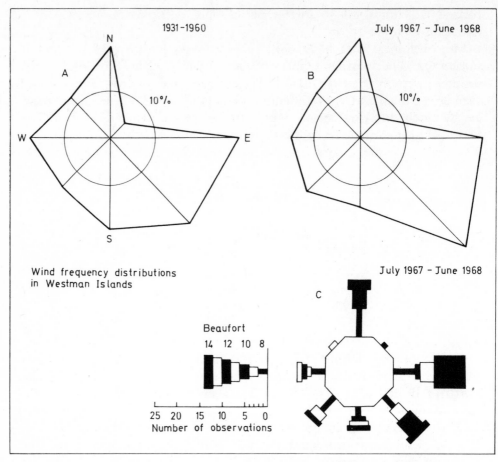

Figure 7.1. Wind frequency diagrams from the Westman Islands (Courtesy: J. O. Norrman)

Similarly, the wind speed is somewhat less than is recorded at Stórhöfdi, but the station there is situated at a higher level than the Surtsey station.

Winds from south-east and east dominate, and the frequency of winds from north-east is at the lowest value because of the shadowing effect of the mountains and the glaciers of Eyjafjöll and Mýrdalsjökull.

A wind frequency distribution for the period 1931 to 1960 at Stórhöfdi is shown in Figure 7.1.

The directions and high velocity of the winds have a marked effect on Surtsey. The strong southerly winds can generate higher waves than the northerly winds, as the fetch is limited by the south coast of Iceland.

The wind and wave action is constantly shaping the island. This can be seen by a comparison of the configuration of the Surtsey maps from various years. Northerly winds are mostly dry, and they may carry dust from the mainland of Iceland. During periods of high winds salt spray commonly sweeps over the whole island.

Although the general climate on Surtsey is similar to that on Heimaey, the micro-climate may be considerably different, both in the black sand and the various sheltered hollows of the lava. In spite of high precipitation, conditions are quite arid in most parts of the Surtsey substrate. No fresh water can be found on the island except in small hollows of rocks, while the lagoons which contained brackish water have been filled up both by silt and sand.

REFERENCES

NORRMAN, J. O., 'Trends in postvolcanic development of Surtsey island, Progress report on geomorphological activities in 1968', *Surtsey Res. Progr. Rep.*, **5**, 95–113 (1970)
SIGTRYGGSSON, H., 'Preliminary report on the results of meteorological observations on Surtsey 1968', *Surtsey Res. Progr. Rep.*, **6**, 119–120 (1970)
The Meteorological Bulletin, *Vedráttan*, 1944–1962, Reykjavik

8

THE ORIGIN OF LIFE

And where the soft air of the heat met the frost so that it thawed and dripped, then, by the might of that which sent the heat, life appeared in the drops of running fluid . . .

The Deluding of Gylfi

THE EMERGING ELEMENTS

In volcanic areas the earth's crust is relatively thin, usually considered to be 30 km, or there is glowing magma in chambers at a relatively small depth, under the crust's surface. There the glowing magma is under pressure. And as the magma enters the surface its various gas components are liberated. First the gases are released as small bubbles that later may combine into larger pockets, as the pressure becomes lower with the rising of the lava to the surface. The stream of bubbles from the magma through the water causes an upwelling of sea surface during the early phases of the eruption and later produces the splashing of the lava fountains. The gas which is liberated may differ in composition due to the difference in solubility of the various components and the time of release from the melt. It has been estimated that the magma contains 0.9% water by weight at 1100 °C, most of which is released as the magma cools down. It has been considered of great value if the other components of the gases could be measured. This was performed successfully during several occasions on Surtsey. The gases were collected at various sites, such as at cracks in cooling lava where they could be tapped by a tube as they were emitted from a lava stream, or where they escape under pressure through openings in the roof of a lava vein, or through chimneys or hornitos formed on the solid lava crust above the magma. Some of the samples were actually contaminated with air, but on other occasions the samples were almost free of inactive gases, indicating complete absence of air contamination (*see* Table 8.1).

The gases collected under such conditions at Surtsey may be considered to be among the purest ever retrieved from a hot magma, and they should be

Table 8.1. *Volcanic gases from Surtsey*

Gas	Percentage		
	I	II	III
H_2O	86.16	86.16	86.16
HCl	0.40	0.40	0.43
SO_2	3.28	1.84	2.86
CO_2	4.97	6.47	5.54
H_2	4.74	4.70	4.58
CO	0.38	0.36	0.39
N_2	0.07	0.07	0.07
CH_4	0.00	0.00	0.00

a fair sample of volcanic gases. Such gas contains mostly water, but also sulphur dioxide, both carbon dioxide and carbon monoxide, as well as hydrogen and hydrogen chloride.

However, the gases released during the earlier stages of the eruption may have differed from those that were sampled. During the explosive phase the light gases, which may have collected in the upper section of the magma, were presumably released first. In this initial phase the composition of the magma was also somewhat different than at later stages, due to a differentiation in the magma in which the two main components of the basalt tend to separate as the olivines sink, while the plagioclases tend to float.

During various eruptions in Iceland fluorite has been emitted through the craters with the ash in the early stages of volcanic activity. This was not encountered in the Surtsey outbreak. However, it has to be borne in mind that the amount of sea-water coming in contact with the magma is tremendous, so that the low fluorite-measurements in the sea around Surtsey do not exclude the possibility that fluorite was present during the initial phase. Like other volatile materials, it could have been dissolved in the water, as the gases were emitted through the sea and could have been precipitated. Although a study of the nutrient content of the ocean around Surtsey during the first months of the eruption did not indicate this emission, it is known that fumaroles often emit an appreciable amount of hydrogen fluoride, as well as hydrogen chloride and ammonia.

The analysis of samples of sea-water from the Surtsey area, however, revealed that there had been a significant increase in phosphate, and especially that a pronounced enrichment in reactive silicates had taken place in the sea-water within 30 km of the eruption centre.

The fine tephra that emanated during the explosive phase of the eruption may have contained some amount of nutrients, already in a comparatively soluble form. These were likely washed out when the tephra particles rushed through the sea-water. A part of the tephra never reached the ocean surface, part rained down from the column and clouds, and some eroded from the island into the sea, so the tephra was repeatedly in contact with the water. The dissolution of nutrients was still further increased by the high temperatures of the water in the crater and the large surface of the small ash particles. During later phases of the eruption the glowing lava flooded down from the island into the ocean, and dissolution from the lava may again have taken place.

Thus it was demonstrated on Surtsey that both gases and various nutrients were released. And, in a similar way during all volcanic activities on our planet, the cooling magma has gradually released various elements and in that way built up the present atmosphere and ocean.

WAS LIFE PRODUCED?

Many have speculated about what conditions may have prevailed on primitive earth to trigger the genesis of the first, simple organic compounds.

If we are to simulate in our mind the conditions existing in the cradle of life, we can only rely on some of the natural forces that still exist on our planet. Although life may be a universal phenomenon, a rather uncommon chain of events may be required for its genesis. The necessary prerequisite for the synthesis of an organic compound is the presence of raw materials in an available form and some source of energy for bringing about the chemical reaction. The required energy may have been in the form of heat, electricity, or radiation. The primordial synthesis of biological molecules may have taken place in the primitive atmosphere, and later the molecules were dissolved in water or, what is more likely, the cradle of life was in the ocean or a crater lake where the raw materials were found in water solution. Just as the interphase between air and water is a possible place for a chemical synthesis and a site for some linking up of atoms, even greater is the chance of a reaction at the interphase between molten lava and ocean water, where a solution loaded with inorganic nutrients is brought to a sudden boil. A submarine eruption provides all the possible combinations of elements and forces that might be required for such an organic synthesis. And if such a reaction did take place during an eruption in primordial times—why could not the same conditions as well have been provided on Surtsey in our days? An ingenious medieval metallurgist with a vivid imagination would never have dreamed that such a Plutonic atmosphere, as hovered over Surtsey, could exist on earth. Just as it will be difficult for today's scientist to imitate all the variables provided in the natural laboratory of Surtsey with its energy supplied by numerous lightnings striking a vapour cloud loaded with suspended nutrients, or the glowing lava with a temperature of 1100 °C sizzling in the ocean broth. During the time of the Surtsey eruption several attempts were made to ascertain whether any organic compounds of abiogenic origin were being produced.

Scientists from the United States National Aeronautics and Space Administration visited the island and collected fresh ash which was falling from the crater island, Syrtlingur. The ash was collected before and after it touched the surface of Surtsey. The scientists also sampled dry and wet surface dust from Surtsey and from crater fumaroles with temperatures ranging from 120 °C to at least 150 °C. In the ashes from Surtsey some amino acids were found, the presence of which was extremely interesting. However, it could not be concluded that they were of abiogenic origin, as there were a number of possible sources of contamination, such as from the ocean floor, the sea-water, and the atmosphere through which the ash and gases were ejected during eruption. But it was worth noting that the amino acids analysed in the ash were not the same as those found in the sea-water around the island. This evidence seemed to suggest an abiogenic origin of the amino acids found on the ash particles.

I had previously suggested the possibility of controlling the conditions and processes which might cause the synthesis of amino acids, if an experiment could be performed in such a way that contamination from living sources could be excluded, or kept at a minimum. Using this as a basis, I proceeded with a simple experiment, letting molten lava fall into samples of water in the following way. Three different kinds of liquids were prepared: distilled water, filtrated sea-water, and a salt solution made by dissolving various inorganic salts in distilled water to produce artificial sea-water. The liquids were both sterilised in an autoclave, filtrated through Zeiss-filters and kept in sterile containers in cool storage. Three gallons of each sample were then used in the experiment, and one gallon of each kept as a control. In the course of the experiment there were also used two ladles with long shafts and three aluminium vessels of 20 litres' capacity.

During an expedition to Surtsey on 14 October 1966, it was possible to get access to and obtain molten lava in an isolated opening approximately 500 m

Figure 8.1. The author scooping hot lava for the experiment to detect formation of organic molecules

from the crater, where the magma with a temperature of 1100 °C flowed in subterraneous veins or closed tunnels from under the solidified surface of somewhat older lava (Figure 8.1). The solid lava surrounding the open fissure was free of any vegetation, as Surtsey was almost devoid of life at that time and there seemed to be little chance of any contamination from the air.

The molten lava was now scooped up with a ladle from the magma stream and poured into three aluminium vessels, each containing a different kind of liquid. Approximately a 6 lb portion of magma was scooped into each container. When the molten lava came in contact with the liquid an explosive boiling occurred, with steam being emitted for at least five minutes. During the sudden contact between the molten lava and water, a charge-separation is generated and the temperature of the solution increases rapidly. Should the proper elements for a synthesis be present, the chances are that they might combine into simple organic compounds. And precisely by this experiment it could be demonstrated that the solutions which had been in contact with the hot lava contained several amino acids, especially large traces of glycine and alanine. This and other experiments strongly suggest that abiogenesis does not necessarily have to be confined to the primordial conditions on primitive earth, but rather that a synthesis of simple organic compounds can take place wherever conditions may be similar to those present at that time. Such conditions may exist during volcanic activities, especially in submarine eruptions.

On Surtsey the basic compounds required for the synthesis were available in solution or in the form of gases, and the energy necessary for producing such a genesis was available in forms of temperatures as high as 1000 °C and electricity that even caused lightnings. Scientists regard oxygen to have been almost, if not entirely, absent from the primitive atmosphere. But oxygen-free conditions are also found during volcanic outbreaks. Should these have been the conditions necessary for the primordial formation of life, the very similar conditions at Surtsey may also have produced a synthesis of primitive organic compounds.

A genesis of life may after all be a more common phenomenon than hitherto accepted. And a spontaneous generation may at any time be a frequent and an inevitable process on our planet. The fate of the simple organic compound which may be formed in this way is not necessarily a simultaneous breakdown, nor is it likely that these compounds will form a basis for an evolution of new organisms. However, if they are of the L-series of configuration, they undoubtedly become a building material for various organisms that are almost always present somewhere in the neighbourhood. Thus any free amino acids which might be synthesised in this way are instantly attached to larger molecules and engulfed by some living bodies.

REFERENCES

ANDERSON, R. *et al.*, 'Electricity in volcanic clouds', *Science*, **148**, No. 367, 1179–1189 (1965)

BJÖRNSSON, S., 'Electric disturbances and charge generation at the volcano Surtsey', *Surtsey Res. Progr. Rep.*, **2**, 155–161 (1966)

BJÖRNSSON, S., BLANCHARD, D. C. and SPENCER, A. T., 'Charge generation due to contact of saline waters with molten lavas', *Jour. Geophys. Res.*, **72**, No. 4, 1311–1323 (1967)

FRIDRIKSSON, S., 'Possible formation of amino acids when molten lava comes in contact with water', *Surtsey Res. Progr. Rep.*, **4**, 23–29 (1968)

PONNAMPERUMA, C., YOUNG, R. S. and CAREN, L. D., 'Some chemical and microbiological studies of Surtsey', *Surtsey Res. Progr. Rep.*, **3**, 70–80 (1967)

SIGVALDASON, G. E. and ELÍSSON, G., 'Report on collection and analysis of volcanic gases from Surtsey', *Surtsey Res. Progr. Rep.*, **2**, 93–97 (1966)

SIGVALDASON, G. E. and ELÍSSON, G., 'Sampling and analysis of volcanic gases in Surtsey in 1966', *Surtsey Res. Progr. Rep.*, **3**, 96–98 (1967)

SIGVALDASON, G. E. and ELÍSSON, G., 'Sampling and analysis of volcanic gases at Surtsey', *Surtsey Research Conference, Proceedings*, Reykjavik, 69–70 (1967)

SIGVALDASON, G. E. and ELÍSSON, G., 'Collection and analysis of volcanic gases at Surtsey', *Surtsey Res. Progr. Rep.*, **4**, 161–163 (1968)

STEFÁNSSON, U., 'Influence of the Surtsey eruption on the nutrient content of the surrounding seawater', Sears Foundation: *J. Marine Res.*, **24**, No. 2, 141–268 (1966)

9

ECOLOGICAL ASPECTS

The ash is the best and greatest of all trees, its branches spread out over the whole world and reach up over heavens. The tree is held in position by three roots that spread far out . . .

The ash Yggdrasil endures more pain than men perceive, the hart devours it from above and the sides of it decay, Nidhögg is gnawing from below.

The Deluding of Gylfi

The biota of various islands differ widely in origin, richness and composition. Distant islands which may be hundreds of kilometres from other landmasses are often rich in endemics, if they are of ancient geological origin. Islands of more recent origin are often poor in species and have but a few endemics. Those which have undergone recent denudation or have recently emerged from under the ice or out of the sea are ecologically poorly advanced.

Biologically such islands are interesting subjects and, due to their simplicity in species, are well suited for basic ecological investigation. In the following chapters a few of these ecological aspects will be dealt with that concern some of the biological problems in Iceland, including that of the Westman Islands and the most recent member, the new-born volcanic island of Surtsey. There one may compare the conditions of smaller islands with those of the larger ones, and primitive communities with the complex and more advanced in succession. However, in order to understand the ecological problems on Surtsey a brief account should first be given of some general biological aspects concerning Iceland.

THE ICELANDIC BIOTA

Most of the Icelandic fauna must have dispersed to Iceland in post-glacial time. The birds which have been recorded as seen are of 230 species, of which 75 species nest in Iceland and only 30 species are permanent residents; the others migrate to the south in winter. Of mammals only the fox, mouse, rat, reindeer and mink live wild, and all but the fox have been introduced. Salmon, brook-trout, char, eel and stickleback are found in lakes and rivers, but there are no reptiles, and no ants or mosquitoes among the 900 species of insects which have been found in the country.

In the post-glacial flora of Iceland there are approximately 430 species of vascular plants. This assembly of species and communities is in accordance with the climatic conditions of the country, which is subarctic to arctic, but at the same time oceanic with relatively mild winters, moist and windy.

It has been commonly accepted by many Icelandic botanists that more than half the species in the indigenous flora have survived at least the last glaciation. This element of the flora is considered to have reached the island by a land-bridge, connecting Iceland with the continent of Europe, during the last interglacial period, and then survived the last glaciation as small refugia on nunataks and other ice-free regions, while the greater part of the country was covered by glaciers. The remainder of the species in the present Icelandic flora must accordingly have reached Iceland in post-glacial times.

This theory is partially supported by the fact that a number of species seem to have a centric distribution corresponding to regions which, according to some geologists, might possibly have remained ice-free during the last glaciation.

An earlier opinion was that Iceland had been completely covered with ice and that all species in the present biota would have to have dispersed post-glacially over the ocean.

At present, it will be difficult to prove either theory. But if it is assumed that half the number of species in the present flora could have dispersed to the island over the ocean, one might therefore just as well argue that a greater part of, or even all the species, could possibly have come in that way, across the ocean.

The Icelandic biota must, for instance, be young in the country, as no true endemic species are encountered. Neither is the centric distribution necessarily an indication of glacial survival. The species may have a centric distribution due to a late sporadic immigration or because of certain environmental conditions at the centric locations, favouring certain elements of the biota there. Thus, in the north central mountain ridge alpine–arctic species predominate. In the south central region the temperate element is found, and so on. These centres have definite environmental boundaries.

Since the time of the settlement of Iceland 1100 years ago, man has greatly influenced the vegetation of the country. There were no herbivorous mammals in Iceland prior to the settlement, and the vegetation may be considered to have been in perfect balance with other natural forces. However, with the introduction of domestic animals there was a drastic change in the biotic harmony and an upset of the equilibrium which the vegetation had reached with the environment. Cultivated plants and weeds were introduced, some of which spread rapidly and invaded the native communities. Ever since there has been a sporadic introduction of species. Since the turn of this century, for example, 190 new accidental introductions of vascular species have been recorded. In addition, deliberate plant introduction is made by the various gardeners, the Agricultural Research Institute and the *Iceland Forest Service*.

Many of the introduced species of plants and animals have become well established and may be considered permanent members of the present biota, whereas others are dependent on rather artificial man-made habitats and have only become temporary immigrants.

It is obvious that a greater number of species than those that were present in the original native Icelandic biota are able to survive in the country.

The poverty of species is to some extent caused by the recent geological origin of Iceland or recent emersion from the glacial dome, as well as by the edaphic and climatic conditions, the latter being rather selective due to the subarctic location of the country. But the oceanic barrier and the distance from the source of available species must also have affected greatly the quantity of species in the native biota. There are, for example, no plants with burs or bristles that have been dispersed by mammals. The oceanic barrier as a selective factor in dispersal can to some extent be studied on islands which have previously been devoid of life. New volcanic islands, such as Surtsey, offer favourable conditions for this kind of research.

ECOLOGICAL STUDIES ON SURTSEY

When discussing the subject of colonisation of biota on the island of Surtsey, many interacting factors have to be considered, such as: (1) the location of the territory; (2) the source of available species for dispersal; (3) the means of dispersal; (4) landing facilities; and (5) living conditions on the island.

As Surtsey is an island in the North Atlantic Ocean, it already occupies a special position which primarily limits a great number of possible colonisers of the island to arctic and subarctic species. Secondly, the invading biota has to be transported over an ocean barrier, which again obviously excludes a vast number of species that might otherwise have a chance to colonise the island, for instance those species that depend exclusively on dispersal by land animals. The colonisation of Surtsey is in that respect not comparable to isolated areas on land or areas with similar substrata on the mainland, such as new lava flows or barren sand stretches, to which plants can be carried attached to terrestrial animals, or to which they might be blown by rolling over a land surface., or simply to which they could spread by vegetative growth. The colonising plants on Surtsey have to overcome greater obstacles and a more selective barrier.

The amount of living material dispersing to Surtsey should be roughly in proportion to the distance of source of available species. This might, however, be biased by some special and local conditions, such as strong air and ocean currents and the selective long-distance dispersal by migratory birds. Surtsey is one of a group of islands, the nearest being Geirfuglasker (Great Auk Skerry) at a distance of 5.5 km. It is reasonable to consider this and the other outer islands to be the most likely habitats from which biota could colonise Surtsey. A thorough examination of the biota of these individual islands is thus a necessary prerequisite to such an investigation. Should their individual biota vary in number of species, the survey enables a determination of the minimal distance a species has to be transported in order to reach Surtsey. This again reflects the spreading potentiality of various species.

A dispersal from the mainland of Iceland is also extremely probable, where the vegetation of the southern part has an obvious advantage over the more arctic element of the interior and the northern districts. Finally, there is the possibility of a long-distance dispersal. This would most likely be from other European countries, though America and other sources should not be excluded.

Although the study of the colonisation of Surtsey is of great interest *per se*, it could thus also furnish information on the long-distance dispersal of plants and animals in the North Atlantic basin and give valuable answers to many a riddle in the great confusion and dilemma of the argument between those who believe that all life was completely eradicated in Iceland during the last glaciation, or the *tabula rasa* theory, and those who believe that life in Scandinavia and Iceland survived the last glaciation on ice-free centres or nunataks.

REFERENCES

FRIDRIKSSON, s., 'On the immigration of the Icelandic flora', *Náttúrufr.*, **32**, 175–189 (1962)

LÖVE, A. and LÖVE, D., 'Studies on the origin of the Icelandic flora', *Rit Landbún.*, B–**2**, 29 (1947)

STEINDÓRSSON, s., 'On the age and immigration of the Icelandic flora', *Societas Scientiarum Islandica Rit*, **35**, 157 (1962)

10

WAYS OF DISPERSAL

When they were going along the sea-shore, the sons of Bor found two trees and they picked these up and created men from them.

The Deluding of Gylfi

The major ways of plant dispersal to Surtsey are by air or ocean currents. Plants could also be transported by various drifting objects, by birds and possibly by other animals, and finally by man.

The dispersal by air of lower plants to Surtsey has been measured on various occasions by counting colonies on agar plates. By this route both bacteria and moulds are brought with air currents. Similarly, spores of ferns, mosses and lichens will be able to disperse by wind. However, seeds of vascular plants equipped with plumes for wind dispersal have also been noted. Once a shower of small fruits of the common groundsel, *Senecio vulgaris*, came drifting on the air like an invasion of parachutists. These fruits very likely came from the mainland rather than from the smaller islands. Similarly, in the autumn of 1971 and again in 1972 there was an airborne invasion of the nuts of cotton grass, *Eriophorum scheuchzeri* (Figure 10.1). These must have been carried from the mainland of Iceland, as *Eriophorum* is not found on the smaller islands and the small colony of cotton grass on Heimaey did not produce seed. Only the light seeds and those equipped with bristles for the purpose will be conveyed in this way to the island, and it is evident that such a dispersal is quite selective towards a limiting number of species capable of air dispersal.

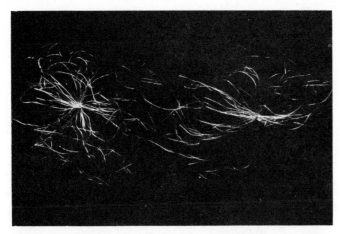

Figure 10.1. The hairy seeds of the cotton grass, Eriophorum scheuchzeri, *are dispersed by air and were first found in Surtsey in 1971*

Figure 10.2. Looking for seeds and other diaspores within the drift zone

Table 10.1. *Vascular plant species and parts recorded drifted ashore on Surtsey during the summer months in the period 1964–1972*

Species	64 Vegetative parts	64 Seeds	65 Vegetative parts	65 Seeds	66 Vegetative parts	66 Seeds	67 Vegetative parts	67 Seeds	68 Vegetative parts	68 Seeds	69 Vegetative parts	69 Seeds	70 Vegetative parts	70 Seeds	71 Vegetative parts	71 Seeds	72 Vegetative parts	72 Seeds	The outer islands	Heimaey	The mainland
Achillea millefolium	x																		x	x	x
Agrostis tenuis	x	x																	x	x	x
Alopecurus pratensis					x		x													x	x
Angelica archangelica		x		x															x	x	x
Anthoxanthum odoratum	x																		x	x	x
Armeria maritima	x						x				x					x			x	x	x
Atriplex patula		x			x		x														x
Betula sp.									x												x
Cakile edentula		x		x	x	x				x				x					x	x	x
Calluna vulgaris					x				x		x		x		x				x	x	x
Carex maritima							x					x									x
Cerastium caespitosum													x						x		x
Cochlearia officinalis	x						x		x		x		x		x		x		x	x	x
Elymus arenarius		x	x		x		x				x	x	x	x	x		x		x	x	x
Empetrum nigrum							x		x		x		x							x	x
Equisetum arvense									x		x		x						x	x	x
Euphrasia sp.	x																				x
Festuca rubra	x		x		x		x		x	x	x		x		x		x		x	x	x
Galium boreale	x								x						x				x	x	x
Hippuris vulgaris	x							x											x	x	x

60

Table 10.1. (continued)

Species	64 Vegetative parts	64 Seeds	65 Vegetative parts	65 Seeds	66 Vegetative parts	66 Seeds	67 Vegetative parts	67 Seeds	68 Vegetative parts	68 Seeds	69 Vegetative parts	69 Seeds	70 Vegetative parts	70 Seeds	71 Vegetative parts	71 Seeds	72 Vegetative parts	72 Seeds	The outer islands	Heimaey	The mainland
Honckenya peploides							x			x		x	x	x						x	x
Juncus balticus	x				x																x
Ligusticum scoticum	x																				x
Matricaria maritima	x		x		x		x		x				x		x	x	x		x	x	x
Mertensia maritima	x									x			x			x			x	x	x
Poa pratensis	x		x		x		x						x		x		x			x	x
Poa trivialis							x												x	x	x
Polygonum viviparum		x																		x	x
Puccinellia maritima					x		x												x	x	x
Rumex acetosa					x														x	x	x
Saxifraga caespitosa																	x		x	x	x
Scirpus caespitosus					x																x
Sedum acre									x		x									x	x
Sedum rosea	x						x		x	x	x								x	x	x
Silene maritima	x						x			x									x	x	x
Stellaria media							x		x						x	x				x	x
Taraxacum acromauris					x												x			x	x
Trifolium repens																				x	x
Bryophyta																	x			x	x
Lichenes							x										x			x	x

The species is found on

61

Dispersal by ocean is the most likely way of invasion, and obviously the marine bacteria, moulds and algae have the advantage there. However, the seeds and other diaspores of vascular plants found drifted on the shore of Surtsey already make up a long list (Figure 10.2). As early as 14 May 1963 wilted leaves and stems of *Elymus arenarius* and *Juncus balticus* were observed in the debris, and seeds of the following species were collected: *Elymus arenarius*, *Angelica archangelica* and *Cakile edentula*.

At the same time green plants of *Sedum rosea* and *Matricaria maritima* were discovered on the shore. A plant of the latter species which had drifted on to the shore was successfully kept alive in a pot for some time, which shows that diaspores other than seed can disperse to the island and start growth. Similarly, stolons of *Elymus arenarius* can withstand the ocean transport and start to develop on the sandy habitat of Surtsey.

In Table 10.1 are listed plants which have been recorded on the shores of Surtsey. The plant list covers mainly the observations through spring and autumn. These diaspores are mostly found after heavy storms, but during long periods of calm weather hardly any diaspores drift ashore, and during some summers there has been very little drift of living material to the island.

Most of the species listed are found growing on the outer islands: some that do not grow there must have dispersed over longer distances. The remaining species on the list are either found growing on Heimaey, or on the mainland of Iceland.

Species common on the neighbouring islands are most abundant in the drifted material, which indicates that the incidence of dispersal is mostly influenced by the distance from source of plant material and its available quantity. Thus *Cochleria officinalis* and *Festuca rubra* are frequent in the drifted material, both being common species on the neighbouring islands as well as on Heimaey. Parts of *Betula pubescens*, *Empetrum nigrum* and *Hippuris vulgaris* must have derived from the mainland of Iceland, as these species do not occur on the Westman Islands. Parts of such species can easily be carried from the interior down the rivers and then drift over to the islands as seeds or other floating plant parts. It is interesting to note that seeds of *Cakile edentula* are found among the debris in most years, although that species does not grow permanently on the island. It remains difficult to explain why this species, which had been most abundant on Surtsey the first year, does not colonise every year.

The dispersal by ocean to Surtsey is affected by the direction of surface winds and sea currents, by the buoyancy of the seeds and other plant parts and by the ability of seeds to retain their germination ability after immersion in salt water. In order to understand fully the possibility of ocean dispersal to the island it is thus necessary to note the speed and directions of the currents around Surtsey. Having obtained information on such factors it is possible to estimate whence and at what time seed could drift to Surtsey. In an experiment which was performed in order to determine the survival period of seed in sea-water, it was demonstrated that seeds of a number of Icelandic species keep their germination ability for a long time after such treatment.

Seeds from three coastal plants and three alpine plants were collected. The seeds were stored in covered glass flasks containing sea-water at 2 °C. At regular intervals 25 seeds were removed from each flask, washed in fresh water and their germination ability tested. The results obtained are shown in Table 10.2.

It should be noted that the seeds of all the coastal species had not fully emerged from dormancy when the experiment started. Their germination ability was therefore low during the first weeks, but increased gradually as

Table 10.2. *Percentage of germinating seed following storage in sea-water at 2 °C.*

Species	Percentage germinating per weeks in sea-water						Salinity %
	I	2	4	8	16	32	
Silene acaulis	70.3	100.0	92.1	84.0	57.0	42.3	3.18
Cardaminopsis petrea	82.2	38.4	15.6	52.0	52.0	0.0	3.12
Cerastium alpinum	100.0	91.3	46.7	90.0	90.0	74.0	3.12
Matricaria maritima	6.6	10.0	30.0	24.1	40.0	54.5	3.26
Plantago maritima	5.1	20.0	66.7	72.0	72.0	50.5	2.61
Cakile edentula	0.0	30.0	20.0	60.0	85.4	37.5	3.27

time advanced. At the end of a four month period the salt water had produced only minor changes on the viability of the seed. At the end of an eight month period the viability of the seed began to decrease, and *Cardaminopsis petrea* had apparently completely lost its germination ability. In Table 10.2 the salinity of the sea-water is recorded in the last column. Salinity had increased slightly from the original 3.09% due to evaporation of water. The deviation, however, does not exceed that of normal variation in salinity of the ocean surrounding Iceland.

After immersion for eight months most of the species tested showed 40–70% germination, indicating that many an Icelandic species could easily disperse from the mainland by ocean to Surtsey. During that time they might even disperse between continents and retain their germination ability.

The buoyancy of seed is of value for ocean dispersal, but this character of the seed is not essential for its ability to disperse by ocean, as seed can float attached to all sorts of driftwood, debris and ice. As an example of such a long-distance dispersal, it should be sufficient to mention here the case of the floating ice island of Arlis II, which carried a few species of plants from the Arctic towards Icelandic waters in 1965.

Table 10.3. Seeds from mermaids purses of the skate, Raja batis

Sample no. of purses	Species of seed	Quantity of seed per purse	Notations
1	*Agropyron repens*★	6	
2	—	8	
3	—	2	
4	—	6	
5	—	1	
6	—	3	
—	*Elymus arenarius*	1	
7	*Agropyron repens*	1	empty spikelet
—	*Phleum commutatum*	1	
8	*Elymus arenarius*	1	
9	*Agropyron repens*	1	
10	*Elymus arenarius*	1	immature caryopsis
11	*Agropyron repens*	1	
12	—	3	
13	*Elymus arenarius*	2	
14	*Agropyron repens*	35	
—	*Elymus arenarius*	3	
15	*Agropyron repens*	1	
16	—	2	
17	—	1	
—	*Alopecurus geniculatus*	1	
18	*Agropyron repens*	4	
19	—	4	
—	*Elymus arenarius*	2	
20	*Agropyron repens*	4	
21	—	18	
—	*Carex sp.*	1	infertile seed
22	*Agropyron repens*	14	
—	*Elymus arenarius*	4	
—	*Alopecurus geniculatus*	1	
23	*Agropyron repens*	3	
—	*Elymus arenarius*	7	
—	*Alopecurus geniculatus*	1	

Total number of seeds	131	Average number of seeds per purse	5–6

★ Some of the *Agropyron* seeds resembled those of *A. trachycaulum*, but they are probably all *A. repens*.

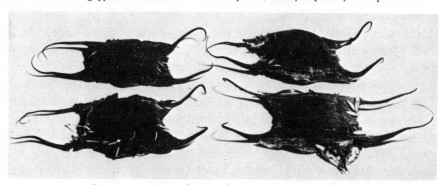

Figure 10.3. Mermaids purses from Surtsey covered with seeds

The landing facilities on an island are a further problem in means of dispersal. In that respect Surtsey differs from most of the outer islands in having low sandy beaches favouring the landing of drifting seeds. One would, therefore, expect the ocean route to be the most plausible way of dispersal of seed to Surtsey.

The colonisation of the coastal plants, now growing on Surtsey, definitely proves that diaspores have dispersed successfully to the island in this way.

MERMAIDS PURSES AS DISPERSERS OF SEED

During the summer of 1969 the shores of Surtsey were regularly searched and records made of the drifting diaspores, but rather few seeds were discovered. It was, however, noted that during May a number of 'Mermaids purses', the capsulated egg of the skate *Raja batis*, had drifted ashore. When these were inspected, a number of seeds were observed attached to the rough outer surface of the 'purses'. The chitinous material of the purses was somewhat shredded into thin bristles to which the seeds adhered. Some of the seeds were hairy, which still further increased the adhesive effect. The seeds found on the purses were identified and counted. They are listed in Table 10.3 according to species and quantity of seed per purse (Figure 10.3).

Except for one infertile fruit of *Carex*, the seeds found attached to the mermaids purses were all of grass species common in Iceland. These were *Agropyron repens*, *Elymus arenarius*, *Phleum commutatum*, and *Alopecurus geniculatus*. However, only *Elymus arenarius* is found growing on the smaller islands of the Westman archipelago. But all are found growing on the largest island, Heimaey, as well as on the mainland of Iceland. All but *Phleum commutatum* are, for example, found on the southern coast near the village of Stokkseyri.

It must be presumed that the seeds and purses came into contact on some neighbouring coast, where the seeds became attached, and from where they were dispersed to Surtsey. The shortest possible distance of dispersal for this collection of seeds that were attached to the purses is that between Heimaey and Surtsey, a distance of 20 km.

It has long been known that fish may eat seeds and thus take part in their dispersal. Darwin experimented with the feeding of seed to fish, and some seeds are used as bait with which to lure fish. On the other hand, it has not previously been known that fish eggs can also act as dispersers of seed.

Other animals are a further means of seed transportation. Among the mammals, seals have been seen on Surtsey, but it is doubtful whether they carry any diaspores to the island. The birds which frequent the island are a better means of transport.

DISPERSAL BY BIRDS

As previously stated, distant islands must to a great extent owe their plant and animal life to long-distance dispersal of living material. The role played by birds has long been in dispute among biologists.

The almost sterile habitat of the new volcanic island of Surtsey offers a unique opportunity to study the possible role of birds in transporting plants and lower animals across wide stretches of ocean.

Sea-gulls are constantly soaring above Surtsey and various sea-birds inhabit or visit the island. Similarly, many migratory birds land there during their flights between Iceland and the more southern countries of Europe. Any of these birds may, to some extent, act as carriers of small organisms and disperse plants and animals to Surtsey.

Thus it has been observed that some of the vascular plants that are now growing on the island have definitely been brought in by sea-gulls. In many cases the plants have grown out of bird droppings or bird carcasses, in other cases, however, no definite assertion can be made.

The birds which have now started to nest on Surtsey will probably carry plant material to their nesting grounds, and could in that way transport diaspores to the island.

Their nests will then serve as incubation areas for various smaller organisms which will enjoy shelter, heat, and the fertile soil provided by the birds. These spots will become colonisation centres for such organisms. Some of the migratory birds caught on Surtsey have had parasites, both in their alimentary tract as well as on the exterior of their body. Beetles have been discovered in their throats and these in turn may also host parasites. Some of these organisms may spread among the local bird population and become inhabitants of the island.

In order to study freshwater biota on Surtsey, some traps were set up in the form of sterile laundry tubs. The rain-water gradually filled up some of these tubs, and they were thus frequently visited by birds that used the water for drinking and bathing. After two years of exposure up to 25 different species of lower organisms were found in some of these traps, and there was a green tinge of algae on the sand in the near vicinity of some of the tubs, bird feathers, droppings, and even some vascular plants. Many of these organisms must undoubtedly have been transported by birds. In addition to these observations on the part played by birds in dispersal of organisms, it was noted that birds carry various smaller organisms and parts of tissues on their feet. Feet of 90 migrating birds, caught after having landed on Surtsey, were inspected for organisms. On thirteen individuals various species of diatoms and spores of moulds and mosses were discovered, as well as filaments of moulds and parts of tissues of higher plants.

The sea-gulls of Surtsey undoubtedly bring the diaspores from the neighbouring islands, but a long-distance dispersal may possibly be effected by some of the migratory birds.

BIRDS AND SEED DISPERSAL OVER LONG DISTANCES

Surtsey, being the southernmost territory of Iceland, has become the first landing place for migratory birds arriving in the spring from European countries. Thus, migration of birds to the island was recorded and a variety of birds were collected on Surtsey as they arrived. Such an investigation started during the period 31 March to 12 May 1967. The birds caught were identified, sexed and weighed. They were then closely examined for any possible seeds or other organisms which might be attached to the exterior of the body, after which the birds were dissected and their alimentary tract cleaned of content. If there were seeds present, they were identified and tested for germination. Finally, the grit from the gizzard was inspected, as minerals or rock types so found might reveal where the last intake of food occurred.

Of the total number of 97 birds of 14 different species, none of the birds carried seed on their exterior. A few birds carried nematodes and other parasites. Of the total birds caught, 32 were snow buntings of the nominate race, *Plectrophenaz nivalis nivalis*, which is not native to Iceland but migrates via Iceland to Greenland from the British Isles and which differs from the Icelandic race. Of these, 10 individuals had seeds in addition to grit in their gizzards. The 10 birds carried with them 87 seeds, the majority of which seemed viable. Plants from two seeds were grown to maturity (*Polygonum persicaria* and *Carex nigra*).

The records indicate that only the snow buntings of the nominate race were seed carriers. That the seeds were in the gizzard and none in the stomach indicates that the birds had not been caught feeding, but had apparently consumed the seeds at an earlier time. The accompanying rocks and minerals definitely show that the birds had not been on the mainland of Iceland, i.e. there was no old Icelandic basalt in the gizzards. On the other hand, there were grains of cinder picked up in Surtsey and rock types and younger sediments which must have been collected by the birds outside Iceland.

Most of the seeds identified from the gizzards were of species rather common both in Iceland and the British Isles, such as crowberry, *Empetrum*, a rush, *Scirpus*, and a member of the pink family, *Spergula*, as well as the sedge, *Carex nigra*, also *Polygonum persicaria*, a European species, which only survives in Iceland near cultivated areas.

One seed was identified as bog-rosemary, *Andromeda polifolia*. This plant is definitely not found growing in Iceland, but is native to Greenland as well as the British Isles, where it is found in bogs from Somerset to the Hebrides. A few seeds are with hesitation identified as those of alfalfa, *Medicago sativa*. If this is correct, it would almost eliminate both Greenland and Iceland from being the place of origin of the seeds. It is concluded that the seed in the gizzards of the snow buntings, together with the mineral grit, were either

Table 10.4. *Number of seeds found in samples from snow buntings caught on Surtsey in 1968*

Kind of seed	Bird no.				Total per kind
	12	13	68	110	
Silene (vulgaris?)	2	I	2	I	6
Carex nigra	I	—	3	—	4
Total seeds per bird	3	I	5	I	10

picked up by the birds in the British Isles and carried by them over the ocean to Surtsey on their migration to Greenland via Iceland, or picked up in Surtsey with the Surtsey ash. Should the former statement be true, it would prove that birds transport seed over long distances and some seeds retain viability.

In 1968 the capture of emigrating birds was repeated. Three assistants stayed on the island during the period 16 April to 10 May and collected over 200 birds of various species.

The birds were dissected and their alimentary tracts cleaned of content. This content was then inspected for organisms, when seeds were present, these being classified and tested for germination. The grit from the gizzard was inspected for minerals which might reveal its origin and thus the possible location of the last food intake.

Of the 200 birds caught, only five were snow buntings of the same nominate race. Four of these birds were found to carry seeds in their alimentary tract. As in previous years, the seeds were found in the gizzard. No other birds carried seeds. In Table 10.4 the numbers of seeds obtained are listed.

The 10 seeds discovered were of two species. Six were identified as seed of *Silene* species, possibly that of *S. vulgaris*, which is a recent introduction to Iceland found growing in cultivated areas, but the seeds might also possibly be of the species *S. maritima* which is common in Iceland. Four seeds were those of *Carex nigra* (*C. fusca All.*, *C. goodenowii Gay.*), which is a sedge common to Iceland. When tested for viability, one of the *Carex* seeds germinated and grew to the seedling stage. Seed of this same species was also found in the snow buntings caught on Surtsey in 1967.

The grit accompanying the seed in the gizzard was exclusively that of Surtsey ash. Contrary to the discovery of metamorphic rock-types and younger sediments accompanying the seed in the snow buntings of 1967, only light-brown glassy tuff particles from Surtsey were found in the snow buntings of 1968. However, there was not any old Icelandic basalt among the grit either, which indicates that the birds had not recently been on the mainland of Iceland.

From that year's results nothing definite can be stated about the origin of the seed found in the snow buntings. The two kinds of seeds discovered are of species which are found growing in Iceland as well as in neighbouring countries. The observation, however, supports the previous discovery on Surtsey that snow buntings are most likely to be carriers of seed. Also, that the seeds discovered were either carried by the snow buntings from the European countries in the south over the ocean to Surtsey on their migration to Greenland via Iceland, or, which is also possible, that the seeds as well as the Surtsey ash were picked up in Surtsey by the birds. Should the seeds have been picked up in Surtsey, they would previously have had to drift to the island. Whichever was their way of dispersal, the discovery shows that the seed of these plants can reach the island by dispersal and that both *Polygonum persicaria* and the *Carex* seeds at least retain their germination ability following such a dispersal.

REFERENCES

EINARSSON, E., 'On dispersal of plants to Surtsey', *Surtsey Res. Progr. Rep.*, **2**, 19–21 (1968)

FRIDRIKSSON, S., 'The possible oceanic dispersal of seed and other plant parts to Surtsey', *Surtsey Res. Progr. Rep.*, **2**, 56–62 (1966)

FRIDRIKSSON, S., 'Source and dispersal of plants to Surtsey', *Surtsey Research Conference, Proceedings*, Reykjavik, 45–50 (1967)

FRIDRIKSSON, S., 'Records of drifted plant parts on Surtsey in 1968', *Surtsey Res. Progr. Rep.*, **5**, 15–18 (1970)

FRIDRIKSSON, S., 'Seed dispersal by snow buntings in 1968', *Surtsey Res. Progr. Rep.*, **5**, 18–20 (1970)

FRIDRIKSSON, S., 'Diaspores which drifted to Surtsey 1969', *Surtsey Res. Progr. Rep.*, **6**, 23–24 (1972)

FRIDRIKSSON, S., 'Mermaids purses as dispersers of seed', *Surtsey Res. Progr. Rep.*, **6**, 24–27 (1972)

FRIDRIKSSON, S. and JOHNSEN, B., 'Records of drifted plant parts in Surtsey 1967', *Surtsey Res. Progr. Rep.*, **4**, 39–41 (1968)

FRIDRIKSSON, S. and SIGURDSSON, H., 'Dispersal of seed by snow buntings to Surtsey in 1967', *Surtsey Res. Progr. Rep.*, **4**, 43–49 (1968) also in 'Plants and Gardens' (*Brooklyn Botanic Garden Record*), **25**, No. 4, 54 (1969–70)

II

SUBSTRATE

The necessary prerequisite for an effective colonisation by pioneer plant invaders of a bare area is the presence of favourable substrata. Characteristic of the substratum of Surtsey is its volcanic origin and its extremely low water retention capacity. The substrata are mainly of three types; the lava, the tephra, and the secondary beach substratum.

THE LAVA

Under normal circumstances the formation of soil on Icelandic lava is an extremely slow process.

On the east and south side of Surtsey there is lava of varying age, the older part being covered by a thin layer of volcanic ash and cinder which has filled hollows and crevices. This cinder substratum may accelerate the formation of soil on the Surtsey lava, but these dry and bare substrata without any organic material are extremely hostile habitats, and it will presumably take some time for biota to accomplish there a successful establishment. The first invaders of the lava are mosses and lichens which form the primary lithosere.

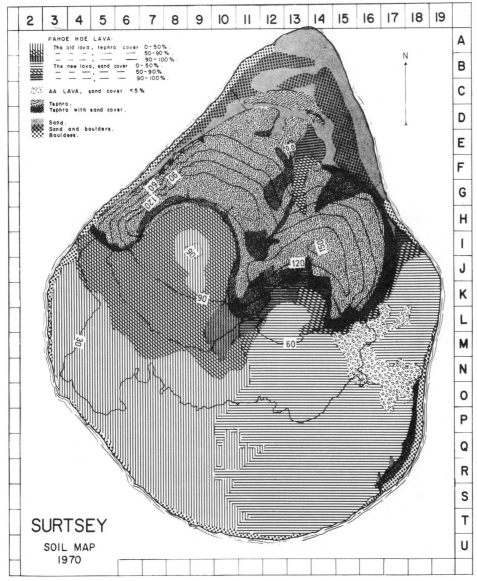

Figure 11.1. A substrate map of Surtsey showing the areas of different kinds of lava, the tephra and the sandy shore

THE TEPHRA

The central part of the island is largely formed of loose tephra which will later harden into tuff. This substratum was formed during the first phase of the eruption and was continuously mixed with ocean water. When tested for soluble mineral content, it still had a high salt content (2.850 mg/l of Cl in the leachate). This substratum is still practically sterile.

Lyme-grass, *Elymus arenarius*, may possibly be the first to establish itself in the dry sand forming the primary psammosere. Only time will show in this respect.

THE BEACH

On the beach of Surtsey, however, conditions favourable for plant growth can develop rapidly. Organic material is washed ashore, e.g. seaweed and driftwood, as well as the remains of various marine organisms. This organic matter mixes with the washed-out volcanic cinders, and gradually decomposes. Large numbers of sea-birds frequent the shore, supplementing the organic content of the sand with their excreta. This initial step in the formation of soil on the beach, however, is not stable. The heavy winter seas cause considerable disturbances to such an extent that material deposited is churned up, thus changing the stratification of the soil.

The most soluble nutrients are washed away, while other organic matter is buried by sand and shingle. Although a great deal of organic matter is thus lost, the sea compensates with a fresh supply of drift material. This cycle is repeated annually, so there is no question of a really stable formation of soil on the shore. However, some organic matter may be carried up the beach beyond the highest tide-mark and thus supply the basis for a more consistent soil formation with an improvement in water retention capacity. Such conditions now exist on the northern shore of Surtsey, where some of the primary invaders of vascular plants on the island are growing.

A substrate map of Surtsey, Figure 11.1, made from an aerial photograph taken in 1970 and observation on the island, using twelve categories shows further details of the distribution of the various substrates.

REFERENCES

FRIDRIKSSON, S., SVEINBJÖRNSSON, B. and MAGNÚSSON, S., 'Substrate map of Surtsey 1970', *Surtsey Res. Progr. Rep.*, **6**, 60–64 (1972)
SIGVALDASON, G. E. and FRIDRIKSSON, S., 'Water soluble leachate of volcanic ash from Surtsey', *Surtsey Res. Progr. Rep.*, **4**, 163–164 (1968)

12

COLONISATION

Thanks to the thorough observations on Surtsey and the detailed recordings of biological events which were started shortly after the island was formed and have continued ever since, it has been possible to study closely the colonisation by various organisms, and to follow the numerous attempts at establishment with all its failures and sometime successes.

Earlier in this book an account was given of the first attempts of individuals to colonise the island. These included both higher and lower forms of life; plants and animals, that are common in the ocean around the Westman Islands and on the islands of the archipelago. The invasion of these organisms has taken place both on the socle of the island, as well as on the dry land of Surtsey, with the result that parts of the volcanic cone are now, after ten years, spotted with vegetation and various colonies of animals. It has been pointed out that the rate of dispersal of biota to the island is directly proportional to the abundance of available material and roughly inversely proportional to the distances from the source of available colonisers; also the mobility of the life form is obviously an important factor.

A successful colonisation, however, does not take place unless the conditions are favourable on the island for the new arrival, so that it can withstand the limitations extended by the edaphive and climatic factors. So far, there is hardly any competition on the dry land of Surtsey between the newly invaded plants. But the conditions on the island have been so stringent that only the most tolerant species have succeeded in getting established.

It is generally believed that lichens are the first invaders of a bare area and that they may be followed by moss, which, in turn, is invaded by grass. These are also the first stages of succession in rock and gravel habitats and some lava fields in Iceland. However, on Surtsey bacteria, moulds, algae and vascular plants were discovered before any moss or lichens were observed. Three years passed until moss started to grow on the lava, and it was only during the eighth year that the lichens started to colonise. This is mainly due to the fact that Surtsey is a relatively small island with sandy beaches containing organic material, washed ashore by the ocean, such as seaweed and the remains of birds and marine organisms (Figure 12.1). Although these beaches are unstable habitats, they were more favourable for an invasion than the dry lava and the scouring tephra.

The ocean around the island has been the main route of transport for seed of various coastal plants. Such seed is constantly being washed upon the shores, and it was inevitable that some coastal plants would be among the first pioneers. Thus the ocean has favoured the colonisation on the beach to a greater extent than on inland lava and tephra, but the pioneers on the beach are also subject to the great erosive effect of the ocean on their habitat, and are, therefore, less protected and not as stable as the inland colonists.

Although the beach was the first habitat to be colonised, the pioneer vascular plants there have not increased to the same extent as the inland plants. The moss on the inland lava flows is thus definitely the most pronounced plant colonist of Surtsey for the time being. The same difference in selection applied for most of the animals that visited Surtsey or were dispersed to the island by air or ocean. For these individuals the beach was the most frequented area. There organic material was available for birds and various invertebrates and lower animals. On some occasions the beach has become covered with *Euphausids*, which have been washed ashore, and which in turn have served as a food source for various kinds of birds, insects and lower organisms. In many ways the shore on Surtsey thus soon resembled any other Icelandic coastline.

In order to facilitate a better orientation during various investigations on the island, a team of surveyors proceeded in 1967 to fix a co-ordinated system onto a map of Surtsey and to select quadrats representing four typical substrates. For this purpose, certain points were established throughout the island. These were later marked by conspicuous marks (sandbags) for aerial photography. The Surtsey map was in that way connected with co-ordinates 05 and 42 in the Icelandic co-ordinate system. Squares, each one hectare in area, were then drawn on the map and identified by a letter and a number,

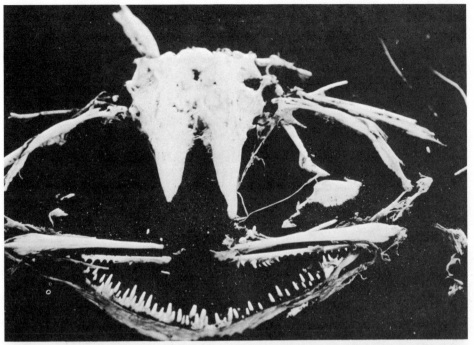

Figure 12.1. *Organic matter is constantly being washed upon the shore and carcasses are deposited in the sand. (Top) A skeleton of a frog-fish,* Lophius piscatorius, *and (Bottom) a dead kittiwake,* Rissa tridactyla, *serve as energy sources in the ecosystem of Surtsey*

e.g. A1, B2, etc. The north shore was closely surveyed according to this system and the corners of the squares were marked with iron pipes. This co-ordinate system has been used extensively as an aid in locating the various sites of study on the island. Following the survey of the island, four fixed quadrats were selected for a more detailed study. These are according to the map identified by letters and figures as D11, F15, K18 and J3.

D11 lies to the north-west of the hut and extends over a low ridge, Bólfell, 10–20 m above sea-level, where meteorological instruments have been installed. The substratum is of the loose tephra type, similar to that found in the neighbouring hills and formed in the earliest phase of the eruption.

F15 is east of the southern lagoon. Within the quadrat is an area once covered by the older lagoon, though the greater part of this has since been filled up by sand and lava. The quadrat is on a level platform of sand about 6 m above sea-level. The substratum is washed-out beach sand mixed with various kinds of drift material.

K18 lies on the eastern margins of the new lava, which is bare and has not been overlaid with cinder.

J3 is in the north-western area of the older lava, about 150 m from the sea and 16 m above sea-level. The area is level for the most part, though with a slight slope towards the west. The basis is ropy-type lava with a 10 to 15 cm overlay of ash. The ash, deriving from the eruption of the smaller islands Syrtlingur and Jólnir, filled all hollows and crevices in the lava, and may therefore accelerate the formation of soil.

These quadrats were selected to provide as wide a variety of growth conditions as possible on the four types of substrata, i.e. washed-out beach sand; loose tephra and ash, which hardens to tuff; bare, recent lava; and older lava with a surface-layer of ash.

REFERENCES

FRIDRIKSSON, S., 'The colonisation of the dryland biota on the island of Surtsey off the coast of Iceland', *Náttúrufr.*, **34**, 83–89 (1964)

FRIDRIKSSON, S., 'Life and its development on the volcanic island, Surtsey', *Surtsey Research Conference, Proceedings*, Reykjavik, 7–19 (1967)

FRIDRIKSSON, S., 'Life arrives on Surtsey', *New Scientist*, 28 March, 684–687 (1968)

FRIDRIKSSON, S., 'The colonisation of vascular plants on Surtsey in 1968', *Surtsey Res. Progr. Rep.*, **5**, 10–15 (1970)

FRIDRIKSSON, S., 'Colonisation of life on remote islands', *NASA Technical Memorandum*, **X–62, 009**, 20–22 (1971)

FRIDRIKSSON, S. and JOHNSEN, B., 'The colonisation of vascular plants on Surtsey in 1967', *Surtsey Res. Progr. Rep.*, **4**, 31–38 (1968)

13

MARINE
RESEARCH

From the blood which welled freely from his [Ymir's] wounds they fashioned the ocean, then they put together the earth and girdled it, laying the ocean round about it. To cross it would strike most men as impossible.

The Deluding of Gylfi

During the volcanic eruption the cinder cone built up from a depth of 120 m and covered an area of 6.5 sq. km, of which 2.8 sq. km were above water. The smaller satellite volcanoes added each approximately 1 sq. km to the submarine base of the Surtsey structure. This cinder pile with the lava crust which, during the latter part of the volcanic activity, flowed down its southern side, covered and destroyed all the benthic organisms of a part of the sea floor. At the edges of the submarine cone the layer of ash gradually thinned out and its effect dwindled. The ash, however, reached as far out as one nautical mile off the island, where a thin layer of ash was measured over a layer of mud. This had somewhat affected the benthic life, and fewer animals were obtained there during dredging in April 1964 than sampled at a station farther away.

The phyto- and zoo-plankton around the island, however, had not been affected. This was demonstrated by numerous samples taken from the ocean around the island during special surveys in the months following the beginning of the eruption, and with the aid of the continuous plankton recorder of the M/S *Gullfoss* that passed Surtsey every third week during the first winter and every other week during the summer.

The mechanical activities of the tephra, pressure during explosions and high temperatures, undoubtedly influenced locally the pelagic life at the site of eruption, but the effects were minimal some metres out. During the first oceanographic survey in the area that took place on 15 to 16 November 1963, no increase in sea temperature was, for example, noticed at a 300 m distance from the eruption centre, and various surveys that followed revealed the same findings. This was especially noticeable during the period of tephra formation. When lava started to flow into the sea there was, however, some rise in temperature. In July 1964 a temperature of 30 to 40 °C was once recorded at 50 m distance from the edge of the lava. But in general the effect of the eruption upon the sea-water was negligible. The salinity was not changed and there was only a slight increase in some nutrients, which may have been due to greater turbulence near the island and a reduced biological uptake.

THE MARINE ALGAE

Marine algae were among the first plants to drift to Surtsey. Knotted wrack, *Ascophyllum nodosum* were occasionally washed ashore during the first summer of the island's existence, and a few pieces of thallus from *Fucus inflatus* and *Fucus vesiculosus* were recorded as well on the beach in 1964. But during that first year no macroscopic benthic algae had yet attached to the recently developed, naked substrate. Lava was still flowing towards the south, but on the north-eastern part of the island the edge of the lava flow was already broken up into boulders which had rolled towards the sand on the northern ness. On this 'older' lava, which at that time was four to five months old, microscopic organisms were getting settled. There were some marine bacteria, and diatoms which on closer study were identified as *Navicula mollis* and *Nitzschia bilobata*. These were pioneers of the marine benthic vegetation of Surtsey.

In the summer of 1965 some filamentous green algae had been added to the marine flora of the island. These algae, which proved to be *Urospora penicilliformis*, grew as isolated tufts in pure population at the high tide level on a lava cliff at the western side of Surtsey. The sandy beach to the north, on the other hand, seemed to be an unsuitable habitat for the benthic biota, nor did dredging on the lava sea floor at 15 to 20 m depth south of the island show signs of life. Thus, pioneers of the marine benthic vegetation which had colonised Surtsey, 21 months after the island had emerged, were composed only of diatoms and one species of filamentous green algae.

The rather slow process of colonisation of the marine algae on Surtsey may be considered to be due to the relative isolation of the island and the severe environmental conditions. The substrate of Surtsey as such was perfectly suitable for a colonisation. This could be demonstrated by transferring stones from Surtsey, placing them in a well-established floral surrounding and observing how organisms would get attached. Such rocks were colonised by eight species of algae within one and a half months. But the dispersal to Surtsey takes a longer time, although there is a luxuriant marine vegetation on the adjacent islands, the nearest of which is Geirfuglasker 5.5 km away, with about 100 species of algae excluding diatoms.

The various marine algae that have washed ashore as driftweeds show that macroscopic fragments can serve as diaspores, but the microscopic spores are also being dispersed by means of sea currents. All the species reaching Surtsey, obviously, do not necessarily colonise its coast. On the other hand, selective immigration has taken place on its virgin substrate.

Thus in the summer of 1966, the rate of colonisation increased markedly and a noticeable zonation was formed in the supra-littoral and eu-littoral regions with three distinct communities. A green belt, 0.50 to 8.30 m wide, of vigorously growing *Urospora penicilliformis* occupied the rocks by the southern lava apron and the boulders on the east coast. The species grew mostly in a pure strand, but in some places the associated species were *Ulothrix flacca*, *Ulothrix pseudoflacca* and *Enteromorpha flexuosa*. Immediately below this belt the species *Porphyra umbilicalis* had established a colony. This was not surprising, as these species are also represented in the algal communities of the adjacent coasts.

Distinct from the green belt and below it, extending down to the lowest part of the initial region, was a zone of brown filamentous diatoms, mainly, composed of *Navicula mollis* forming a dense slippery coating on the rocks. And among these were some young plants of the kelp, *Alaria esculenta*.

It was interesting to note that the pioneer species of this region were again the filamentous benthic diatoms. And it is likely that the first step in the algal succession of similar areas is always a seral stage of diatoms.

The second step is the colonisation of *Urospora mirabilis* at the high-water mark of the intertidal region and *Alaria esculenta* at the lower water mark. The third community had established in the tide-pools of the upper littoral region, where *Petalonia zosterifolia* was the dominant species associated with scattered individuals of such species as *Pylaiella littoralis*, *Ectocarpus confervoides* and *Petalonia fascia*, to be joined in the following year by the species *Acrosiphonia albescens*.

During the year 1967 SCUBA-diving studies revealed that there was a barren belt in the upper part of the sub-littoral region at 3 m depth. Below this was a broad zone of *Alaria esculenta*, which now extended down to a depth of 17 m. At that site there were only young plants 6 to 18 cm long. The optimal depth for this species seems to be 6 m, where the plants were 1 m long at the time.

Table 13.1. *Vertical distribution of species on and off the north-east coast of Surtsey*
(By courtesy of Jonsson 1970)

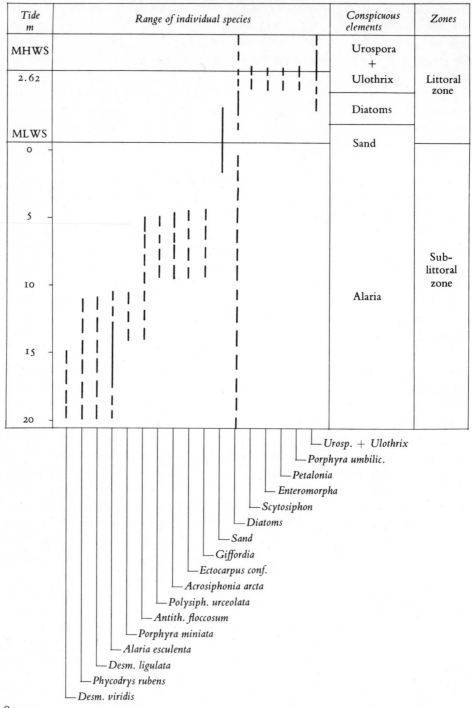

In 1967 there were altogether 17 species of benthic algae discovered growing on Surtsey, excluding diatoms, and in 1968 this figure had increased to 27 species. In the upper part of the littoral region (the littoral fringe) *Urospora penicilliformis* was now found everywhere associated with *Ulothrix* species, and below it on the north-west coast was a belt with *Petalonia fascia* and *P. zosterifolia*, which are subsided by *Porphyra umbilicalis* and *Enteromorpha* species. The upper limit of this belt is at about 1.30 m above low-water mark. Below this, at the lowest part of the littoral region, was the bare belt which, in some places, was occupied by diatoms. In the sub-littoral region *Alaria esculenta* dominated with a cover of up to 80 individuals per sq. m at 12 m depth. Below 10 m depth the *Alaria* was often associated with *Desmarestia* species, *Lomentaria orcadensis* and *Monostroma grevillei*. At deep-water below 20 m there was a scattered vegetation of red algae such as *Porphyra miniata*, *Antithamnion floccosum*, *Phycodrys rubens* and *Polysiphonia urceolata*. The growth of these recent invaders seems to be very rapid. The vertical distribution of species in the various zones as observed on the north-east coast is noted in the accompanying Table 13.1.

The marine vegetation on Surtsey has apparently not yet reached the climax community. But the most common species of the adjacent areas have now colonised on the socle of the island. The new colonisers are all found in the archipelago of the Westman Island except for the species *Porphyra purpurea*, which is new to Icelandic waters.

THE MARINE FAUNA

It has previously been stressed that the volcanic eruption had little effect on the pelagic biota of the ocean around the island. These waters are relatively rich in marine life. And as a matter of fact the banks around the Westman Islands are some of the best fishing grounds in Iceland. During the eruption the fishing continued around Surtsey, and the catch was no less than in the years before.

When walking on the shores of Surtsey, one was repeatedly reminded of the presence of the luxuriant marine animal life. A school of small sole could be seen swimming in the tidal water, and occasionally a few individuals would strand in the sand or be washed ashore. On other occasions a number of lumpfish young would get into the tide-pools and strand, or a red squid might be washed upon the black basaltic sand. Sometimes the shores were literally swarming with *Euphausids* left there by the receding tide.

In December 1963 plankton samples were collected on a transect from one to twelve nautical miles west of the island and again in January 1964, which showed that pelagic animal life was normal and had apparently not been affected by the eruption. During a trawling survey, five and a half nautical miles west of Surtsey, in December 1963 the catch consisted of eight species of fish as well as Norway lobster. This was a further proof that life was normal in the Surtsey waters.

The benthic animals, however, had been destroyed, and while the island was still under formation the colonisation of the benthic animals started.

During the early summer of 1964, I found an odd mussel *Mytilus edulis* on the sand of the south-west coast, which had apparently been brought in with the surf or by a bird. No macroscopic settler could yet be seen. On driftwood and floats from nets that had been washed up on the beach one could observe colonies of goose barnacles *Lepas* spp. that were settling on material foreign to the Surtsey shores, while the primary virgin substrate of the island was not colonised by barnacles *Balanus* until several years later (Plate 10).

In the meantime bottom animals were crawling up the base of the pedestal of Surtsey, and the sediment of sand, sunken pumice and scoria were gradually being invaded by numerous pelagic larvae. The dispersal of these is largely dependent on the distance that the potential parent population has to travel to a new substrate. The longer the distance, the less the chances that the current will bring the larvae to the new habitat.

Already in November of 1964 eight animals were taken by a scraper from a depth of 70 m at 0.2 nautical miles west of the island; two of these were the tube-dwelling worm, *Pectinaria koreni*. The bottom there was rough scoria, and this same substrate reached out to 0.4 nautical miles from the shore, except to the north where the side is mostly gravel. Farther out the bottom was more covered with the finer volcanic material. There, between 0.4 and 1.0 nautical mile, the ash had not seemingly affected the fauna. In 1966 some 100 bottom samples were collected. The species found indicated the presence of the most common animals such as 17 species of marine bristle worms, polychaeta, the most common of which were *Pectinaria* and *Distrupa arietina*. These polychaetes were mostly found at depths greater than 100 m. On the slope, in shallower water, the *Pectinaria* also occurred with other polychaetes such as *Scoloplos armiger* and *Capitella capitata*, and six bivalve species of which the most common was *Abra nitida*, and some starfish, echinoderms, which was represented by the species *Ophiura affinis*. It was remarkable that the polychaetes species should be the first animals to invade the rather barren lava, as they are known to feed on organic contents of the sediment and not on particles suspended in the water. The latter food source was undoubtedly more abundant at that time.

The settlement of these and other animals on the slopes was, however, repeatedly destroyed by deposits of tephra produced by the volcanic islands of Syrtlingur and Jólnir and by later eruptions of lava on Surtsey.

In 1967 most of the life on the slope had thus been killed off. But on the lower levels it had evidently not been affected and seemed to be fairly normal.

Some of this unstable tephra, on the contrary, was to the benefit of marine animals. The pumice produced during the eruption floated on the ocean surface and drifted back and forth over long distances until it was washed upon a far away shore or sank to the ocean floor. During this drifting of the pumice great quantities of the particles served as floats for goose barnacles. The larvae of these animals, which every year swarm the ocean in enormous numbers, suddenly found an unusual opportunity of attachment and means of transport, especially following the pumice production from Syrtlingur in 1965. A cargo of millions of goose barnacles was thus transported towards the Reykjanes peninsula where the load was deposited on the southern shores, or where it became, suddenly, an important item in the diet of the Icelandic sea-gulls. As a matter of fact, this incident was first noticed in the course of an investigation of the feeding habits of sea-gulls, when quite unexpectedly, in the autumn of 1965, up to 70% of their diet consisted of goose barnacles. When an explanation was sought, the shores were found to be covered with pumice carrying barnacles belonging to three species: *Lepas facicularis*, *L. anatifera* and *L. pectinata*. The last named species had not previously been recorded in Iceland. Thus the effects of an eruption can even aid in the dispersal of certain species.

In the following years the sediment on the slopes of Surtsey gradually became more stable and was, in deep water, invaded by the same species as well as new ones of the infauna. Of the worms polychaetes the most common species were again *Pectinaria koreni*, *Spilo filicornis*, *Capitella capitata* and *Owenia fusiformis*. Among the molluscs, the pioneers, were species such as *Abra prismatica*, *Abra nitida* and *Macoma calcarea*. The representatives of crustacea were *Cheraphilus neglecta* and *Hippomedon denticulatus*, and of the echinoderms, the most common pioneer was *Ophiura affinis*. These were associated with a number of species with individuals of less abundance. And, gradually, the communities on Surtsey are reaching the same climax as those of the adjacent islands.

Higher up the pedestal of Surtsey in shallower water, the fauna had some difficulties in colonising due to the continuous fall of ash and flow of lava. The substrate was thus very unstable, and the scouring effect of sharp tephra particles was hard on the juvenile colonists. It was not until the early summer of 1967 that the first barnacle *Balanus* sp. was discovered in a sheltered hollow of the lower part of the littoral region.

In the following years a colony of *Balanus balanoides* formed a zone in between the littoral fringe and the eu-littoral region on the boulders and the cliffs of the southern lava apron of the island. In 1967 SCUBA-divers discovered Hydrozoa on the rocks at 20 m depth, and *Tubularia larynx* was identified in 1968. At the same time species of Nematodes were recorded, and also moss animals, Bryozoa, of which the species *Membranipora membranacea* was most common in the inter-tidal zone. Four species of *Lamellibranchia* with pelagic larvae were discovered in the autumn of 1967 in the inter-tidal as well as the sub-littoral region. The most abundant of these were the saddle oyster, *Anomia squamula* and the common mussel, *Mytilus edulis*. In the sub-littoral region the pioneers of Decapoda were the shrimp, *Spirontocaris pusiola*, and the crabs, *Hyas coarctatus* and *Portunus holsatus*, and in that same year a few species of Copepoda and Amphipoda were also recorded. In addition to this, the SCUBA-divers also observed a number of crabs on the rocky bottom down to 20 m depth, but were unable to identify or catch any of them.

In the following years the tidal region was further colonised by the barnacle *Balanus balanoides* and the common mussel *Mytilus edulis*. These two species obviously predominate in the tidal zone and the region in which the mussel had colonised, extending some distance down in the sub-tidal region.

A comparative study of the benthic fauna of adjacent islands shows that the most common species, in these areas, are gradually colonising the recently formed substrate of Surtsey. Furthermore, the vertical distribution of species found in the numerous samplings so far performed indicates that the classical zonation occurring elsewhere in these areas is also taking place on Surtsey. The most mobile species with pelagic larvae and those that were abundant in the adjacent regions were the first to settle on the pedestal. Some of these species are also known to be especially tolerant to environmental changes, such as variations in temperature, salinity, depth and texture of the substrate. They were thus well equipped to become pioneers on Surtsey. Later arrivals were individuals of less frequent or rare species. By the very intensive study on Surtsey, it has been possible even to discover species which are new to the Westman Islands, such as the barnacle, *Balanus hammeri*, *Calliopius laeviusculus* and the sea squirt, *Ascidia callosa* that were discovered in 1968 and which, as a matter of fact, are new to the south coast of Iceland.

Higher up in the food chain of animals, which so far have occupied the waters around Surtsey and are forming communities in this newly developed habitat, are various species of large and small fish. Thus the capelin, *Mallotus villosus*, passes Surtsey in enormous quantities and is in turn consumed by cod, *Gadus morrhua*, and haddock, *Melanogrammus aeglefinus*. The shores of Surtsey are also frequently visited by seals. Although they have not yet bred on the island, they find this region abundant in food, as do the ocean birds and fishermen.

REFERENCES

The marine algae

HALLSSON, s., 'Preliminary study of the development of population of marine algae on stones transferred from Surtsey to Heimaey 1965', *Surtsey Res. Progr. Rep.*, **2**, 31–33 (1966)

JÓNSSON, s., 'Biologie Marine—le commencement du peuplement benthique des côtes rocheuses du Surtsey, la nouvelle île volcanique dans l'Atlantique Nord', *C. R. Acad. Sci., Paris*, **262**, 915–918 (1966)

JÓNSSON, s., 'Initial settlement of marine benthic algae on the rocky shore of Surtsey, the new volcanic island in the North Atlantic', *Surtsey Res. Progr. Rep.*, **2**, 35–44 (1966)

JÓNSSON, s., 'Premiere séquences du peuplement algal sur les côtes de Surtsey', *Surtsey Research Conference, Proceedings*, Reykjavik, 52–53 (1967)

JÓNSSON, s., 'Further settlement of marine bethic algae on the rocky shore of Surtsey', *Surtsey Res. Progr. Rep.*, **3**, 46–56 (1967)

JÓNSSON, s., 'Survey on the intertidal and subtidal algae in Surtsey in 1967', *Surtsey Res. Progr. Rep.*, **4**, 67–73 (1968)

JÓNSSON, s., 'Meeresalgen als Erstbesiedler der Vulkaninsel Surtsey', *Schr. Naturw. Ver. Schlesw.-Holst., Sonderband*, 21–28 (1970)

JÓNSSON, s., 'Studies of the colonisation of marine benthic algae at Surtsey in 1968', *Surtsey Res. Progr. Rep.*, **5**, 42–52 (1970)

JÓNSSON, s., Marine benthic algae recorded in Surtsey during the field seasons of 1969 and 1970', *Surtsey Res. Progr. Rep.*, **6**, 75–77 (1972)

The marine invertebrates

GUDMUNDSSON, F. and INGÓLFSSON, A., 'Goose barnacles (*Lepas* spp.) on Surtsey pumice', *Náttúrufr.*, **37**, No. 3–4, 222–235 (1967)

GUDMUNDSSON, F. and INGÓLFSSON, A., 'Goose barnacles (*Lepas* spp.) on Surtsey pumice', *Surtsey Res. Progr. Rep.*, **4**, 57–60 (1968)

NICOLAISEN, w., 'Studies of bottom animals around Surtsey', *Surtsey Research Conference, Proceedings*, Reykjavik, 34–35 (1967)

NICOLAISEN, w., 'Marine biological studies around Surtsey', *Surtsey Res. Progr. Rep.*, **3**, 68–69 (1967)

NICOLAISEN, w., 'Marine biological studies of the sub-littoral bottoms around Surtsey', *Surtsey Res. Progr. Rep.*, **4**, 89–94 (1968)

NICOLAISEN, w., 'Studies of the sub-littoral fauna of Surtsey in 1968', *Surtsey Res. Progr. Rep.*, **5**, 63–67 (1970)

SIGURDSSON, A., 'The coastal invertebrate fauna of Surtsey and Vestmannaeyjar', *Surtsey Res. Progr. Rep.*, **4**, 95–107 (1968)

SIGURDSSON, A., 'The benthonic coastal fauna of Surtsey in 1968', *Surtsey Res. Progr. Rep.*, 70–78 (1970)

SIGURDSSON, A., 'The benthic coastal fauna of Surtsey in 1969', *Surtsey Res. Progr. Rep.*, **6**, 91–97 (1972)

SKÚLADÓTTIR, U., 'Report on the marine biological survey around and on Surtsey', *Surtsey Res. Progr. Rep.*, **2**, 67–73 (1966)

14

TERRESTRIAL
RESEARCH

At that time earth will rise out of the sea and be green and fair, and fields of
corn will grow that were never sown. Vidar and Váli will be living, so neither
the sea nor Surt's Fire will have done them injury.

The Deluding of Gylfi

THE BACTERIA AND MOULDS

From the records of diaspores washed upon the shores of Surtsey it may be
inferred that there already existed an organic source of energy on the
island for various bacteria and moulds.

To these records may be added a long list of names of various foreign
items of organic material, which had in the early existence of Surtsey drifted
on to the shore or been carried to the island and could serve as an energy
source for living organisms. The most effective contributors of such an
organic matter were the thousands of sea-gulls which roost on the island and
constantly fly around its shores. Some of the edges of the tephra hills were
already in the first summer white with bird excrements. Another major
energy source was a variety of debris washed up by the sea. This was mostly
confined to the beach, especially to the high-tide level, or a belt marked by
the average tidal amplitude of 2.5 m. On the northern ness this belt has
become increasingly broad. The ness may be completely inundated during
high spring tides and is therefore littered with debris.

This organic matter is mainly in the form of seaweed and kelp or all sorts
of driftwood, logs, tree stumps and boards, but also varieties of carcasses of

birds, fish and other marine animals. To this may be added strings and pieces of nets and all sorts of trash discarded from fishing-boats in the surrounding waters.

All this material is a secondary source of energy in the ecosystem of Surtsey, which may be used by some of the local organisms and which will in a number of ways influence the development of life on the island.

During the summer of 1964 it could be noted that fragments of seaweed and carcasses were decaying at the high-tide mark and were obviously being utilised by bacteria. These processes of breakdown were however not of special interest, and the micro-organisms attacking these organic items would not differ markedly from those found elsewhere on any southern shore of Iceland.

The drifting of debris to the island continues, but there is no marked increase in organic deposit from one year to another. Some of the debris is undoubtedly buried in the sand, other is washed out again, and the carcasses on the shore are immediately cleaned up by the numerous sea-gulls that constantly search the shore for any kind of food.

The primary source of energy in the Surtsey ecosystem is sunlight, which can be utilised by the photosynthetic plants that are gradually colonising the island, but no such plants were available during the first years of the island's existence.

On Surtsey energy was also available as electricity and as thermal energy from the volcanic activity or the energy produced by chemical reactions. Through the catalysis of such energy there might even have been formed some simple organic compounds of abiogenic origin. This primary energy source available for the first micro-organisms of the Surtsey ecosystem was of major interest for the study of the first steps in a biological succession, starting with the colonisation of primitive micro-organisms on the inert substrate and ending with a highly developed climax community containing numerous lower and higher organisms.

Although the shores of Surtsey soon obtained scattered deposits of organic matter of foreign origin, the main part of the island was clean and devoid of these materials, and literally speaking completely sterile at the time of the formation of the island. The substrate was even repeatedly sterilised by the rain of volcanic ash from the eruption of the smaller islands that spread many layers of tephra over most of its original surface. But even a desolated island does not remain free of micro-organisms for any length of time.

The microflora invading Surtsey mainly disperse by ocean and by air. During stormy weather the waves may splash sea foam far upon the island and bring with it various marine micro-organisms. There they will encounter a new environment both regarding salinity and pH. This latter has been found to vary in the top layer of tephra in the range from 4.2

Figure 14.1. Setting up traps for airborne micro-organisms

to 6.5. Some of marine micro-organisms were capable of establishing on the Surtsey substrate, especially in the ocean beach interface. When substrate from the beach was investigated, a number of bacteria and moulds were obtained.

The airborne microflora was measured on Surtsey on various occasions, and the quantity of organisms in the air was compared to that above cultivated and populated areas. These tests proved that there was a constant microbial dispersal by the air currents to the island, but the microflora of the air over Surtsey was scanty in species and low in number of individuals per volume compared with counts in the air of highly developed communities in the adjacent island of Heimaey and on the mainland of Iceland (Figure 14.1). It was noted that direction and velocity of wind affected the quantity of airborne organisms. During northerly winds soil dust was brought from the mainland, and at the same time the air carried an increased number of organisms to the island. Most of the airborne micro-organisms were saprophytes, and no typical animal intestinal bacteria of the coliform group were found when different media were exposed on petri-dishes.

Although micro-organisms were rather easily carried to Surtsey by air, by ocean or even by animals, they have not generally colonised the tephra substrate of the island. The surface of the tephra cones has repeatedly been sampled for such organisms, but although they are present on the surface in small numbers, this substrate was apparently not suitable for supporting micro-organisms because of rather high salinity, lack of organic matter and especially because of the low moisture content.

Despite the precipitation in the Surtsey area being quite high, no rain-water accumulates in any amount on the island but seeps right through the porous substrates, whether it is of lava, tephra or sand. During droughts the surface consequently does not hold sufficient moistures to support the life of micro-organisms.

Where moisture is present, however, both algal and bacterial life has been able to establish itself. Many fumaroles that are still active provide, for example, moisture which condenses in surrounding crevasses. Microscopic examinations of such habitats have revealed a few bacteria per sample. In 1966 rod-shaped forms of very narrow bacteria $< 1\mu$ in a diameter were, for instance, detected growing on a rock in one such fumarole, and in 1970 a direct microscopic examination of the Surtsey substrate showed that bacteria were widely distributed throughout the terrestrial environment on the island. Roots and rhizoids of plants growing on Surtsey all had a high bacterial population. Such bacteria may have been brought to the island attached to the diaspores and are now growing on the organic material excreted by the higher plants.

Some of the habitats on Surtsey are quite unique in respect of diversity and extremes in temperature, such as the fumaroles and the hot areas, which have various gradients of temperature and moisture. There the bacteriologists have observed in small numbers both *Thiobacillus thiooxidans* and *T. ferrooxidans*, whereas denitrifying and nitrifying bacteria were more frequent, but so far tests for desulphurisers have given negative results.

The moulds which are found on roots of higher plants were very likely brought with the diaspores to the island, but mould spores are apparently also dispersing to Surtsey and moulds have been found on enriched media, for example *Penicillium citrinum* and *Phoma putaminum*.

THE ALGAE

The marine algae were pioneer colonisers of the pedestal of Surtsey and became abundant in the littoral region a few years after the formation of the island. In contrast to this the dryland of Surtsey has in general not been colonised by the terrestrial algal species. It has often been suggested that algae are the pioneer plants on a new substrata. This idea is partly based on the discoveries on the volcanic island of Krakatoa, where the blue–green algae were found to be the early colonisers. This, however, has not been the case on Surtsey, and the algal mats which are now found in a few places on the island ten years after its formation are virtually all formed by the coccoid green algae.

Marine algae apparently disperse in great quantities by ocean and can colonise the new substrate within a short time. In contrast, the terrestrial algae do not withstand much salinity, and their dispersal to Surtsey mostly takes place by wind via the air.

It has also been demonstrated on Surtsey that birds carry algal spores and tissues on their feet, and it had even been suggested that insects play a minor part in dispersal of algae.

The transport of terrestrial algae is, however, more restricted than is the dispersal of marine algae via the ocean route. Thus air transport, for example, seems to be selective towards species with small size organisms. This difference in means of dispersal and therefore also in the quantity of capable colonisers is, however, not a sufficient cause to explain the slow rate of colonisation of the terrestrial algae on the dryland of Surtsey, compared to the rapid development of societies of marine algae on the socle of the island.

The variation in the algae population in these two biomes is rather due to a difference in their environmental conditions. Thus, the substratum below sea-level mainly serves as a mechanical support for the organisms, the nutritive matter being available in the salt water, while the terrestrial algae are dependent on nutrition from the dryland substratum. Similarly, the toxic effect of the volcanic salts has been readily washed out of the substrata below sea-level, but may be detrimental to algae in the dryland biome. The erosive effect of the tephra blown back and forth by the wind may be more harmful than similar abrasive effect of tephra which is washed by the waves. The greatest difference in the environment of these two biomes, however, remains in the availability of water. In the terrestrial habitats the substrate, whether it is the solid lava or the loose tephra, is often low in moisture. This periodical lack of water in the superficial substrata of the dryland is apparently the greatest hindrance to the algal establishment, while there is obviously no such water shortage below sea-level.

While various algae are thus rather readily dispersed to Surtsey, they are in general not able to establish or to become dominant plants in the dryland communities.

Compared with the numerous bacteria which have been recorded in the air or on the cinder surface, a wide variety of blue–green algae have been collected on Surtsey and isolated by enrichment culture techniques. The accumulation of these airborne algae is apparently most abundant at the base of the cinder cones, as they may be washed down with rain and carried to lower levels with the run-off water. Thus the greatest amount of blue–green algal species have been recorded at the base of the southern slope of the tephra cones. Altogether over 100 species were recorded in 1968, and over 160 species have so far after 10 years been identified by growing on artificially enriched media from samples collected at these sites. Although the abundance of species may be greatest at this base of the cinder cone and in the sheltered places around the craters, airborne algae capable of surviving have been collected in various surface samples from all over the island, but these are simply not able to establish themselves.

There exist, however, some stable algal settlements on Surtsey, and in a few places layers of algae may be observed. These are, for example, areas on both lava and tephra where roosting birds have supplied fertiliser to the substrate. The colonies at these sites consist almost exclusively of coccoid green algae.

Some algae have also been able to establish where moisture levels are high in crevices of lava, or where steam condenses from fumaroles. On the edges of some such fumaroles the ash particles gradually stabilise, forming a compact, moist crust on which colonies of algae could establish. In 1968 eight species of blue–green algae were recorded in the area of the two central craters, as well as 100 other algal species including 74 diatoms. These were either discovered together or in association with bacteria and mosses, the largest colony being 30 sq. cm in area. The development continued in the following years, and the number of species in the small oasis around the fumaroles increased. These algal settlements, however, have not become conspicuous, and the blue–green algae are quite unimportant as primary colonisers of Surtsey. One exception to this was a wet spot around a bucket filled with rain-water placed on the lava as a trap to attract birds. In this artificial habitat, which received a large amount of bird droppings, a mat of blue–green algae had been formed in 1972, occupied by *Oscillatoria*.

These primary colonisers on Surtsey, however, do not all have to rely on organic supply of nitrogen. Another species of blue–green algae found on the island is *Anabaena variabilis*. This was first discovered in 1968. The following year three *Nostoc* species were also among the algae recorded. These species have the ability of fixing molecular nitrogen. The nitrogen fixation is, however, rather low under the Surtsey conditions compared with warmer habitats, and cannot be considered of major ecological importance in the development of life on Surtsey.

The algal species represented in the microflora of Surtsey are largely identical with the flora of Icelandic soils. The colonists on Surtsey, however, seem to be of species that are of rather small size or are easily transported by spore forms. Although the algae are not necessarily pioneers in the substrate, they are often found in close relationship with the first colonisers of higher plants and are generally represented at the locations occupied by moss.

In the high-temperature areas surrounding steam vents near the old Surtur crater, some of the blue–green algae form a faint green colour. This area is occupied by the thermophilic species *Mastigocladus laminosus*, which grows at temperatures in the range between 57 to 64 °C and in hot springs of alkaline to neutral pH (Figure 14.2). This thermophilic species is a cosmopolitan blue–green algae, which is common in the hot springs on the mainland of Iceland, those closest to Surtsey being at a distance of 75 km. The

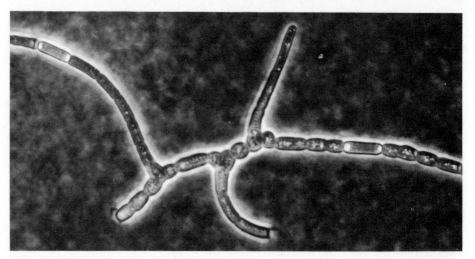

Figure 14.2. A typical branching form of the thermophilic blue–green algae, Mastigocladus laminosus, *which was found growing around some of the steam vents on Surtsey*

inoculum which was transported to Surtsey may have dispersed by air or by birds from these sources. But if precautions are not taken, scientists working in thermal areas may also become agents of dispersal.

THE LICHENS

It is a widely held belief that lichens are pioneer forms of life in the colonisation of new rocky substrata. This is the case with respect to many new lava flows throughout the Icelandic mainland, especially those occurring at high altitudes. It was thus expected that lichen would be an early coloniser of the Surtsey lava. The substrate was therefore thoroughly studied every year following the formation of the island, and birds' feet were investigated to see if they could serve as means of transport for possible lichen colonists.

It was surprisingly not until the summer of 1970 that the first lichen were found on Surtsey. At that time two communities of lichen were, however,

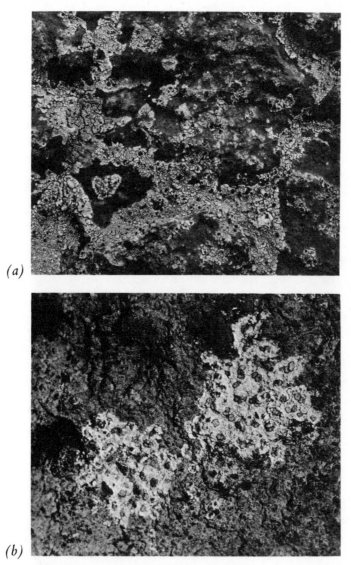

(a)

(b)

Figure 14.3. (a) The lichen, Trapelia coarctata, on the outer slopes of the lava crater Surtur II (Photo: S. Magnússon). (b) The lichen Placopsis gelida (Photo: E. Einarsson) observed in the vicinity of the Surtur II crater. At both sites the habitats received moisture and warm air from a thermal area.

One of these habitats was on a lava crust north-east of the crater. It was occupied by small specimens of *Stereocaulon vesuvianum* a common pioneer lichen on the Icelandic lava flows.

The other habitat was situated on the outer side of the north slope of the crater. This was occupied by two species, *Trapelia coarctata* and *Placopsis gelida* (Figure 14.3). This community was also better developed than the former and covered a strip of several metres in length. *T. coarctata* has not previously been recorded in Iceland but may well be present on the mainland. It is a crustose lichen that was so abundant on the site at Surtsey that it gave the surface of the rock a pale yellowish-brown colour. *P. gelida* was represented by fewer individuals, but this is a common species on post-glacial lava flows in Iceland, so it may be expected that both this species and *S. vesuvianum* will spread out in the Surtsey ecosystem.

In 1971 *Stereocaulon vesuvianum* had obtained a wider distribution and was found scattered throughout the dry lava surface as well as *Stereocaulon capitellatum*. In that same year small colonies of *Acarospora* and *Bacidia* species were also noticed at the Surtur II crater.

In 1972 a bright orange–yellow patch of the species *Xanthoria candelaria* was observed near one of the plastic water tubs. It had apparently been brought there by birds as this lichen is common in Iceland where birds perch, although most of the lichen species on Surtsey must have been carried as soredia by wind to the island, as they are rather evenly distributed throughout the lava flows. Their first appearance at the Surtur II crater is only due to the favourable growth conditions there. In 1973 eleven lichen species had been found on Surtsey.

THE MOSSES

It was not until the middle of August 1967 that the first moss colonies were discovered on Surtsey. These were found on a sand-bank at the northern edge of the New Lagoon. The plants were all of the same species, *Funaria hygrometrica*, and in an early stage of growth. A month later, the second location of mosses was observed at the edge of the central lava crater, where the colonies consisted of two species; *Funaria hygrometrica* and *Bryum argenteum*.

These two moss species, the first to colonise the substrate on Surtsey, are common on the mainland of Iceland. The plants apparently grew from spores that had dispersed to the island by wind and, in the case of the communities at the lava crater, the colonisation became permanent and formed a centre for further establishment of mosses on the Surtsey lava.

(a)

(b)

Figure 14.4. *(a)* *The moss*, Polytrichum alpinum, *on the lava in Surtur II.* *(b)* *The most common moss,* Racomitrium canescens, *on a lava rock* (*Photos: S. Magnússon*)

95

In the following summer three new moss species were found in addition to the already existing moss population on the island. These were *Leptobryum pyriforme*, *Pohlia bulbifera* and *Ceratodon purpureus*.

In 1969 the moss vegetation on the Surtsey lava became more conspicuous with plants occupying the lava in hollows and caverns, where sand had been deposited, and some even settling on the bare lava. The moss was, however, most vigorous where there was heat and steam emission from fumaroles, and where the vapour stabilised the sand and kept a constant moisture in the substrate.

In 1970 the number of moss species on Surtsey had increased to 16, and their distribution had extended into the southern part of the lava apron. The species *F. hygrometrica* and *Racomitrium canescens* were largely responsible for this distribution (Figures 14.4b and 14.7).

The following year 20 new species of mosses were recorded on the island with the total distribution gradually extending over the lava flow. The spread of growth was then mainly towards the west but was hindered on the northern side by the tephra hills. Apparently the tephra was not a suitable habitat for any of the moss species. *Racomitrium canescens* was the dominant species. However, it did not form a heavy cover—only small tufts here and there. In the years 1972 and 1973 the moss cover on Surtsey's lava developed further, but increases in distribution slowed down as compared with its rapid development in previous years, as the most favourable habitats had already been invaded. Other parts of the lava, which have not yet been colonised by mosses, are rather hostile habitats for these plants; some too close to the splashing zone, others too sandy and erosive.

THE SPECIES AND THEIR DISTRIBUTION

On the vegetation maps (Figure 14.5) the gradual development in total distribution may be noted. In comparing the distribution maps with the substrate map, it may be seen that the maximum distribution, which the moss population has reached in 1971 mainly coincides with the lava surface of the island (Figure 14.6).

In drawing the distribution maps, it was decided to use the 100 × 100 m quadrat mesh already used for other studies on the island. The distribution of a species within a quadrat was thus a unit in the total survey.

Since 1967 the moss species have gradually been invading Surtsey and colonising the lava habitats of the island. During our study of the moss population some species have been recorded in one summer and not re-discovered the following year, due to their scarcity in the vegetation. This, however, does not mean that the species could not have been growing

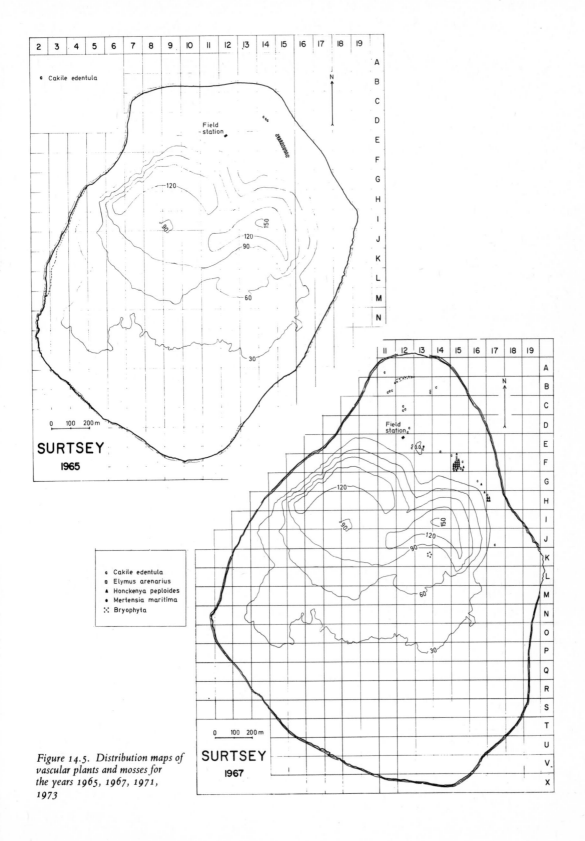

Figure 14.5. Distribution maps of vascular plants and mosses for the years 1965, 1967, 1971, 1973

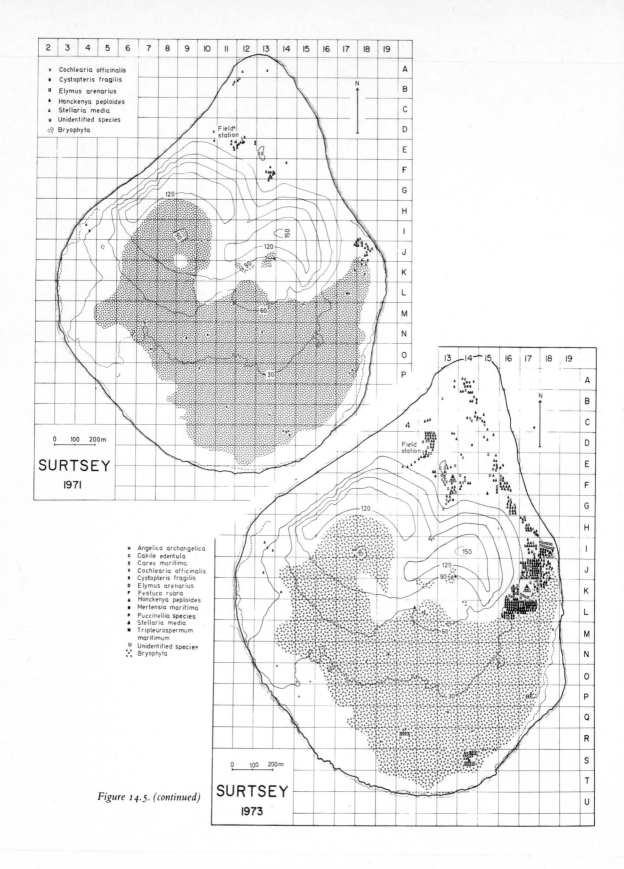

Figure 14.5. (continued)

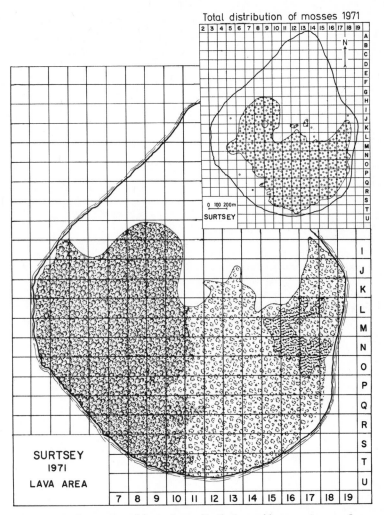

Figure 14.6. Comparison of the total moss distribution and lava area in 1971. Lava in E,F13–14 and G,H13 is omitted

continuously on the island since their first appearance. In other cases a new species has increased so rapidly that its colonisation has been apparent every year. In Table 14.1 are listed the moss species discovered since moss first appeared on Surtsey. The species of moss so far recorded on Surtsey are altogether 69, of which 63 were known to be present in 1972. The greatest increase of species occurred in 1972, when 32 new species were discovered, including three new species of liverworts of the genus Jungermanniales. In the moss flora of the island only some of the species listed are common, others are less common, rare, or very rare. In Table 14.2 the species have been grouped according to four categories, based on their abundance in the

Table 14.1. List of moss species found on Surtsey in the years 1967–1972

Species	67	68	69	70	71	72
Polytrichales:						
Atrichum undulatum (Hedw.) Beauv.				x	x	x
Psilopilum laevigatum (Wahlenb.) Lindb.						x
Pogonatum urnigerum (Hedw.) Beauv.			x	x	x	x
Polytrichum alpinum Hedw.					x	x
Polytrichum longisetum Brid.					x	x
Polytrichum piliferum Hedw.						x
Polytrichum sphaerothecium (Besch.) Broth.						x
Fissidentales:						
Fissidens adianthoides Hedw.					x	
Dicranales:						
Ditrichum cylindricum (Hedw.) Grout						x
Ditrichum heteromallum (Hedw.) Britt.						x
Ceratodon purpureus (Hedw.) Brid.		x		x	x	x
Distichium capillaceum (Hedw.) B.S.G.					x	x
Aongstroemia longipes (Sommerf.) B.S.G.				x		x
Dicranella crispa (Hedw.) Schimp.		x	x	x	x	x
Dicranella heteromalla (Hedw.) Schimp.						x
Dicranella schreberiana (Hedw.) Schimp.					x	
Dicranella subulata (Hedw.) Schimp.						x
Dicranella varia (Hedw.) Schimp.					x	x
Amphidium lapponicum (Hedw.) Schimp.						x
Dichodontium pellucidum (Hedw.) Schimp.				x	x	x
Dicranoweisia crispula (Hedw.) Lindb.						x
Oncophorus virens (Hedw.) Brid.					x	x
Pottiales:						
Encalypta sp.						x
Encalypta ciliata Hedw.					x	x
Trichostomum brachydontium Bruch.						x
Barbula vinealis Brid. var. cylindrica Boul.						x
Barbula fallax Hedw.						x
Barbula icmadophila C.Muell						x
Barbula recurvirostra (Hedw.) Dix.					x	x
Barbula unguiculata Hedw.						x
Grimmiales:						
Grimmia apocarpa Hedw.					x	x
Grimmia maritima Turn.					x	x
Grimmia stricta Turn.					x	x
Grimmia torquata Hornsch.						x
Racomitrium canescens (Hedw.) Brid.			x	x	x	x
Racomitricum heterostichum (Hedw.) Brid.						x
Racomitricum lanuginosum (Hedw.) Brid.				x	x	x

Table 14.1 (continued)

Species	67	68	69	70	71	72
Funariales:						
Funaria hygrometrica Hedw.	x	x	x	x	x	x
Bryales:						
Pohlia annotina (Hedw.) Loeske					x	
Pohlia cruda Hedw.		x		x	x	x
Pohlia proligera Lindb.						x
Pohlia wahlenbergii (Web. & Mohr) Andr.				x	x	x
Anomobryum filiforme (Dicks.) Husn.					x	x
Leptobryum pyriforme (Hedw.) Wils.			x	x	x	x
Bryum spp.		x	x	x	x	x
Bryum angustirete Kindb.					x	
Bryum arcticum (R.Br.) B.S.G.					x	
Bryum argenteum Hedw.	x	x	x	x	x	x
Bryum calophyllum R. Br.						x
Bryum stenotrichum C.Muell					x	x
Bryum pallens Sw.				x	x	
Mnium hornum Hedw.					x	x
Plagiomnium cuspidatum (Hedw.) Kop.						x
Aulocomnium palustre (Hedw.) Schwaegr.						x
Philonotis sp.				x	x	x
Philonotis fontana (Hedw.) Brid.						x
Bartramia ithyphylla Brid.					x	x
Hypnales:						
Drepanocladus aduncus (Hedw.) Warnst.						x
Drepanocladus uncinatus (Hedw.) Warnst.				x	x	x
Calliergon stramineum (Brid.) Kindb.					x	x
Campylium polygamum (B.S.G.) C.Jens.					x	x
Amblystegium serpens (Hedw.) B.S.G.						x
Brachythecium albicans (Hedw.) B.S.G.						x
Brachythecium rivulare (Bruch.) B.S.G.						x
Brachythecium salebrosum (Web. & Mohr) B.S.G.				x	x	x
Hypnum lindbergii Mitt.						x
Rhytidiadelphus squarrosus (Hedw.) Warnst.					x	x
Isopterygium pulchellum (Hedw.) Jaeg. & Sauerb.						x
Marchantiales:						
Marchantia polymorpha L.					x	x
Jungermanniales:						
Cephaloziella sp.						x
Scapania sp.						x
Solenostoma sp.						x

Table 14.2. A list of moss species growing on Surtsey in 1972 grouped according to the four frequency categories

1. Common species: (found in 25 or more quadrats)

Bryum stenotrichum	*Leptobryum pyriforme*
Ceratodon purpureus	*Philanotis fontana*
Dichodontium pellucidum	*Pohlia cruda*
Funaria hygrometrica	*Pohlia wahlenbergii*
Grimmia apocarpa	*Racomitrium canescens*
Grimmia stricta	*Racomitrium lanuginosum*

2. Rather frequent—rather rare species: (found in 6–25 quadrats)

Atrichum undulatum	*Dicranella crispa*
Bartramia ithyphylla	*Distichium capillaceum*
Barbula recurvirostra	*Drepanocladus uncinatus*
Brachythecium salebrosum	*Pogonatum urnigerum*
Bryum argenteum	*Polytrichum alpinum*
Campylium polygamum	

3. Rare species: (found in 2–5 quadrats)

Amblystegium serpens	*Drepanocladus aduncus*
Anomobryum filiforme	*Grimmia maritima*
Aongstroemia longipes	*Grimmia torquata*
Barbula fallax	*Isopterygium pulchellum*
Brachythecium albicans	*Mnium hornum*
Bryum calophyllum	*Plagiomnium cuspidatum*
Dicranella varia	*Polytrichum sphaerothecium*
Dicranoweisia crispula	*Psilopilum laevigatum*
Ditrichum cylindricum	

4. Very rare species: (only found in one quadrat)

Amphidium lapponicum	*Encalypta* sp.
Aulacomnium palustre	*Hypnum lindbergii*
Barbula icmadophila	*Marchantia polymorpha*
Barbula unguiculata	*Oncophorus virens*
Barbula vinealis	*Pohlia proligera*
Brachythecium rivulare	*Polytrichum longisetum*
Calliergon stramineum	*Polytrichum piliferum*
Cephaloziella sp.	*Racomitrium heterostichum*
Dicranella heteromalla	*Rhytidiadelphus squarrosus*
Dicranella subulata	*Scapania* sp. (*curta* or *scandica*)
Ditrichum heteromallum	*Solenostoma* sp. (*atrovirens* or *pumilum*)
Encalypta ciliata	*Trichostomum brachydontium*

Plate 10. Netfloats with goose barnacles were washed upon the sandy beach on Surtsey in 1965

Plate 11. The sea rocket, Cakile edentula, the first vascular plant on Surtsey to flower and set fruits

various quadrats. *Funaria hygrometrica*, which was one of the first moss species to arrive on Surtsey, is also one of the most abundantly and widely distributed members of the moss flora. The *Racomitrium* species arrived somewhat later, but have by now become the most dominant species on the island, especially *R. canescens*, which may also be considered one of the most common species that grow on Icelandic lava flows.

The species *Bryum stenotrichum* is listed in group 1. common species, as it very likely is the main species of the *Bryum* population on Surtsey. However, this cannot as yet be determined, for identification of each sample has not been completed. The various *Bryum* spp. were not fully developed when the samples were taken, and can only be identified by differences in the characteristics of their peristome.

The same is the case with *Philonotis*, of which *P. fontana* is considered the main species representing that genus on Surtsey, although it has not been demonstrated with certainty except in cases of well developed samples. This is also what may be expected, as *P. fontana* is the most common species of that genus in Iceland.

In the last few years there has been a great increase in abundance of the species *Dichodontium pellucidum*, *Leptobryum pyriforme*, *Pohlia cruda*, *Pohlia wahlenbergii* and *Philonotis*. Even more spectacular is the rapid increase of *Grimmia stricta*. During the time between the studies in 1971 and 1972 its frequency jumped from being found only at one site to being the fifth most common species on the island. The same trend can be observed among the related species *Grimmia apocarpa*, which was discovered in only two quadrats in 1971, whereas in 1972 it inhabited 31 quadrats.

THE LOCAL REPRODUCTION OF MOSS

Surtsey's original moss colonisers had to rely on dispersal of spores, which apparently derived mostly from the Icelandic mainland, by air. As the various moss species have become better established, they have gradually developed reproductive organs. In Table 14.3 are listed the species found bearing capsules in 1972, and a note has been made of the quadrat number where the capsule-bearing plants were found.

It is worth noting that the species *Racomitrium lanuginosum* was found bearing capsules on Surtsey for the first time in 1972, when quite a high number of capsule-bearing plants was found in four quadrats. This moss is the most common species on the Icelandic lava flows and will probably also eventually dominate the Surtsey lava. It was slower to invade and mature on the island than many other moss species, but as the capsules have now developed, the species has acquired greater possibilities of spreading.

Table 14.3. *List of moss species with capsules and their location on the island*

Species	Quadrat number
Funaria hygrometrica	Capsules common in many quadrats
Bryum stenotrichum	Capsules common in many quadrats
Dicranella crispa	I8, M5, N14, O7, O11
Grimmia stricta	N17, N18, O17, P9, P10, Q11, Q13
Grimmia apocarpa	L17, M15, N14, I9, N17, N18, O16
Racomitrium lanuginosum	I18, L12, P11, Q12
Barbula recurvirostra	P11
Dicranoweisia crispula	N12

It may also be added that the species *Grimmia stricta* and *Grimmia apocarpa*, which were rather rare in 1971 and have become common in recent years, are both bearing capsules and have thus a local source for spore dispersal.

THE HABITATS

In our studies of the moss vegetation on Surtsey, the various habitats were recorded for each species observed in the different quadrats. The classification was based on 4593 observations. Classical sociological measurements were not applied, as the moss colonies are as yet rather scattered. But the records made give the frequency of the species per quadrat as well as the favoured habitat. The habitat classes, however, were based only on the topography of the lava, substrate, moisture and heat emission, other microclimatic conditions were not investigated.

For evaluation of the habitats, the following categories were used:

1. Perpendicular lava cliffs in hollows and crevices.
2. Moist sand in caverns shaded by a block of lava, from where the condensed vapour drips on to the sand.
3. A thin layer of tephra on the lava surface fully exposed with no effect from fumaroles.
4. Same as habitat 3 but affected by fumaroles.
5. The naked exposed lava surface without sand.
6. Hollows with sand, moist and somewhat shaded.
7. Narrow cracks in the lava filled with sand.
8. Sand, moist and warm from the fumaroles.
9. Sand-covered lava with full light.
10. Sand on a lava slope, partly shaded and with more moisture than in habitat 9.
11. Naked and shaded lava slopes.
12. Sand at the bottom of a deep and narrow crack in the lava.

Table 14.4. *Samples of moss in Surtsey classified according to habitats*

Species	Habitat class*												Total observation
	1	2	3	4	5	6	7	8	9	10	11	12	
Racomitrium canescens	1				954	1	2	1	6	1			966
Bryum sp.	41	124	62	59	25	329	19	10	132	81	5	10	897
Funaria hygrometrica	25	72	23	23	13	274	22		216	82	1	6	757
Racomitrium lanuginosum	15	2			556	4	2	1	2			1	583
Grimmia stricta	13				331	4	5		1				354
Ceratodon purpureus	10	7	4	21	17	64	8	6	90	20	1	1	249
Philonotis sp.	8	5	4	13	2	70	1	4	20	30	1		158
Pohlia cruda	11	5		7	6	40	1		26	16			112
Pohlia wahlenbergii	7	4		6	2	59		5	8	5		1	97
Bryum argenteum		20	21			6			7	5			63
Leptobryum pyriforme	2			7	14	12		1	2	17		1	61
Bartramia ithyphylla	10			3		12			9	5			54
Grimmia apocarpa	4			5	4	20	1		6	7			52
Dichodontium pellucidum	5		2	5	6	2		1	6	5		1	51
Dicranella crispa	5	1	3	14	5	7	1	1	3				40
Pogonatum urnigerum				3		4		1	9				20
Atrichum undulatum	3			3		3			4	3			18
Drepanocladus uncinatus	3				6	2			2	2			16
Campylium polygamum	6				3	1			1	1	1		14
Distichium capillaceum	3				2				2	1			9
Polytrichum alpinum				2		4			2				8
Barbula recurvirostra	3	2								2			7
Brachythecium salebrosum	1	1			1	3							7
Total	176	243	119	191	1988	921	62	31	549	283	9	21	4593

* See text for explanation.

By classifying the species according to their abundance in any one habitat it is possible to show the environment favoured by the species. In Table 14.4, 23 of the most common species are listed according to their dominance in the moss flora of Surtsey, and in such a way that the first species on the list is the most common species on the island, and so on.

The frequency figures indicate how often the species were recorded in the various habitat classes. Thus, for example, the species *R. canescens* was observed altogether at 966 locations being in habitat class No. 5, on the naked exposed lava in 954 of the instances.

From this same Table it can also be seen that some of the habitats are common for various species, while others are only distinctive for one or a few species. Thus, class No. 5 is the most common habitat on the island. It is favoured by various species, such as the two most common *Racomitrium* and two *Grimmia* species. These four species seem to thrive well on the island, but they have not yet had the competition to show which species will eventually dominate in the various moss communities. Several other species were found growing in this habitat. But they are, so far, only associate species in this primary succession. One example of the associate species is *Bartramia ithyphylla* which also grows under various other conditions.

Another common habitat on Surtsey is the sand-covered hollow, classified as No. 6. It is favoured by many species of moss, such as various *Bryum* species, e.g. *B. stenotrichum* and *Funaria hygrometrica*, which are the most dominant species and also a number of associated species, such as: *Philonotis*, *Pohlia cruda*, *Pohlia wahlenbergii* and *Dichodontium pellucidum*.

Other habitats are more rare and have specialised conditions. These are, for example, occupied by species that require more abundant moisture and shading conditions than the common species.

THE COVER

The total cover of moss in Surtsey is still rather sparse and difficult to measure due to the rough surface of the lava. The cover of each species in every quadrat was evaluated in such a way that the present cover was recorded within a 25×25 cm frame at 10 locations within a quadrat. On the maps (Figure 14.7) the cover evaluation is given in average percentages for four common species.

It may be noted that the cover estimates vary according to species and their position in the lava. The species *Bryum* (mostly *B. stenotrichum*) and *Fumaria hygrometrica* have obtained the most extensive cover, the *Racomitrium* being second in coverage. Others have less average cover per quadrat.

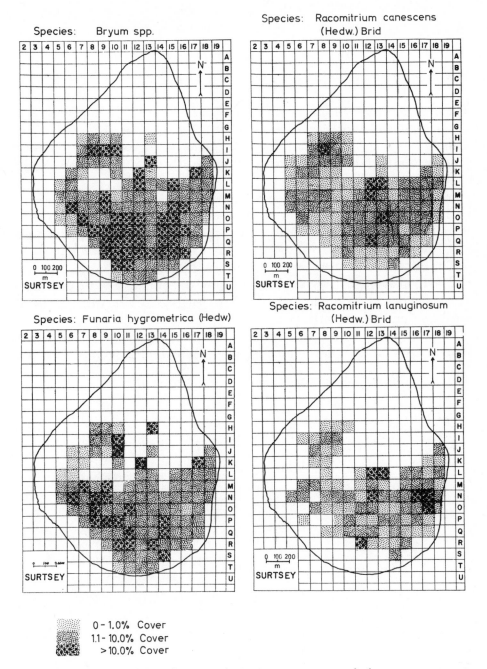

Figure 14.7. Surtsey maps showing the cover evaluation in average percentage for four common moss species

If the distribution and cover maps are compared, it may be noted that cover estimates do not always follow the frequency classes. Where the frequency classes are high the cover estimate is most reliable.

THE BIOMASS OF THE VEGETATION ON SURTSEY AND HEIMAEY

The organic matter produced on Surtsey every year has been negligible so far. In 1971 a quantitative measurement of the biomass of moss was performed in the three quadrats showing the densest cover. The maximum biomass was found in quadrat MII giving an average of 1.020 g/m². Other areas had a much lower biomass.

In the late summer of 1972 the measurements of biomass were continued in the same manner as in the previous year. Samples of moss were collected from the areas that had the densest moss growth. These were sites in quadrats J8 MII and L18.

The calculated biomass from each area is shown in Table 14.5.

The total average in 1971 was 0.518 g/m² as compared with 3.076 g/m² in 1972 and 3.412 g/m² in 1973, so there has been a large increase in the quantity during these three years.

For comparison, measurements of biomass were taken on Heimaey in three different plant communities in 1972. These figures indicate how small

Table 14.5. Biomass of vegetation from Surtsey and Heimaey

	Communities	Quadrat	Average (g/m²)
Surtsey 1971	moss	J 8	0.338
	moss	K 18	0.196
	moss	M 11	1.020
Total average			0.518
Surtsey 1972	moss	J 8	8.671
	moss	L 18	0.096
	moss	M 11	0.460
Total average			3.076
Surtsey 1973	moss	J 8	4.002
	moss	L 18	1.418
	moss	M 11	4.815
Total average			3.412
Heimaey 1972	Meadowland		828.5
	Heath vegetation		898.1
	Puffin-ground vegetation		991.5
Total average			906.1

the biomass of the Surtsey communities is in comparison with the productive and well-established communities on Heimaey.

THE VASCULAR PLANTS

Earlier in this book I have stressed the point that seed and other diaspores of vascular plants drifted to the shores of Surtsey and dispersed to the island by various other means shortly after it was formed and while the volcanoes were still active.

A number of seeds were collected on the shore in 1964 and proved viable and capable of germinating, although no vascular plant started growing during this first summer of the island's existence. But it was considered likely that pioneers of vascular plants would soon be found growing along the shore.

After searching the island thoroughly in the second summer, I discovered the first higher plant on 3 June 1965. Small seedlings of the sea rocket, *Cakile edentula*, were found growing upon the sandy beach north of the small lagoon on the island. During a later expedition in June the same

Figure 14.8. The sea rocket, Cakile edentula, *was the first vascular plant to colonise Surtsey. The picture shows the largest plant with flowers and pods*

year, some 20 additional seedlings of the same species were discovered approximately 50 m east of the previous location.

The plants were all growing in a mixture of tephra and decaying thalli from the seaweed, *Ascophyllum nodosum*, which evidently formed a suitable medium for the germination and growth of the young plants, as the *Cakile* is apparently quite nitrophilous (Figure 14.8). The plants had grown from seed that obviously had been washed ashore, possibly along with the seaweed, which might act as a float, aiding dispersal of seed by ocean.

The seedlings of these pioneer colonists, however, did not mature, and succumbed a few weeks later under a shower of ashes carried from the volcanic crater Syrtlingur. The fall of fresh tephra from this satellite volcano thus delayed the colonisation of higher plants on Surtsey for one year.

The discovery of the *Cakile* plants on Surtsey showed that living seed could be carried by sea at least 20 km, which is the distance from the island to Heimaey, the nearest colony of *Cakile*.

The second attempt of higher plants to invade Surtsey took place during the summer of 1968. On 2 July four seedlings of lyme-grass, *Elymus arenarius*, as well as a seedling of sea rocket were found growing on the sandy shore on the northern side of the island (Figure 14.9f). The plants grew from seeds that had apparently also dispersed by sea, as they were all found growing in a zone at the high-tide line. They were subjected to a similar fate as the plants that had made an attempt to colonise in the year before. This time, however, the colonisers were wiped out by ocean waves sweeping over the low sandy beach.

The summer of 1967 was more favourable for colonisation, and a third species attempted to invade the island. This was the sea sandwort, *Honckenya peploides*, a common perennial on the southern shore of Iceland. During the summer, 26 individuals of this species were recorded, a number of which produced considerable vegetative growth (Figure 14.9a and b). The fourth species on the island was the oyster plant or the lungwort, *Mertensia maritima*, a perennial of which only one specimen was found on the 'New Year' lava by the lagoon (Figure 14.9e). The two former colonisers were also represented. A few plants of lyme-grass were found on the sand and pebbles at the high-tide mark, as well as 21 individuals of sea rocket that grew here and there on the ness, of which 15 flowered and six bore mature pods. Plants of the latter species were thus the first to flower on the island. They set approximately 300 pods with twice as many seeds. The sea rocket was, therefore, first of the colonisers to succeed in multiplying in the new habitat and in laying the foundation for a new generation of plants on the island of Surtsey (Plate 11).

It was therefore surprising that no sea rockets showed up in 1968. The reason for this is not known, but the species is an annual, and neither old

(a)

(b)

(c)

(d)

(e)

(f)

Figure 14.9. *The sea sandwort, Honckenya peploides, on Surtsey. (a) The largest plant of this species with a maximum diameter of 80 cm in 1973. (b) A plant of the same species with fruits. The scurvy grass,* Cochlearia officinalis, *colonised Surtsey in 1969. (c) A young plant on the sand. (d) The largest plant on Surtsey No. 70–74 in quadrat S14 bearing flowers and fruits in 1971. (e) The lungwort,* Mertensia maritima, *a young plant among the debris on the shoreline. (f) The lyme-grass,* Elymus arenarius, *No. 73–400 on the eastern shore of the ness*

plants nor the seed from the last year's crop seem to have survived. The *H. peploides* plants, on the other hand, had increased in number and were now found growing farther up on the lava to the east, where they were better sheltered from the waves and wind in the sand-covered lava. In 1969 still another vascular species was added to the island's flora. This was the scurvy grass, *Cochlearia officinalis*, which is common to the coast of Iceland and is found on the skerries and larger islands in the Westman archipelago (Figure 14.9c and d). Four plants belonging to this species were found growing near one of the plastic barrels filled with rain-water used to attract birds, this being the only source of fresh water on the island. These plants had obviously been carried as seed by birds to the barrels, and it was noted that the plants, beside the barrels, were growing out of bird droppings in association with the algae previously mentioned. The total number of plants found on the island that year was reduced because of a rather unfavourable spring and summer.

On the other hand, some of the *H. peploides* plants had overwintered, and one of these developed 49 flower buds. Most of these sandworts were growing among drifted seaweed on the northern ness, located at the edge of the New Lagoon, which had been filled up by sand during the winter. The fertilisation by the seaweed may, to some extent, have stimulated the growth in this drift zone. On the mainland the sandwort is a pioneer on the sandy shore, particularly on the fore-dune.

In 1970, the major event was the discovery of still another vascular species; the common chickweed, *Stellaria media*. A close scrutiny revealed that there were, in fact, four plants growing together in a compact bunch out of a sand-filled lava crack. Around them were fragments of shells, bird droppings and feathers, and it was obvious that the plants had grown up from the droppings of a bird. These plants matured and set 12 fruits. Some of the seeds ripened and dispersed from the plants during late summer. This year the scurvy grass plants had also increased in number. These had apparently also grown from seed that birds had carried to the island.

An exceptionally large percentage of vascular plants survived the winter of 1970 to 1971, or 40 out of 75, and only a few were added, so the total number reached 57 individuals. Both that winter and spring were unusually mild, and as most of the plants had been growing in the rather sheltered parts of the ness and up on the lava edge to the east, they had a better chance to overwinter than individuals in previous years.

In extensive areas of the lava, an increased amount of tuff and ash had drifted in from the tephra mounds. At first the sand accumulation in the lava had mainly taken place in the old lava on the western side and consisted partly of tephra from the island of Jólnir, but gradually the lava became filled up by drifting sand from the eastern edge of the coastal plain as well as

Figure 14.10. (a) Red fescue, Festuca rubra, *in quadrat L12, the only plant of this species on the island. (b) The grass,* Puccinellia maritima, *in quadrat R14. (c) The sedge,* Carex maritima, *No. 70–72, see also Figure 18.3. (d) The bladder fern,* Cystopteris fragilis, *No. 72–113 in a hot crevice by the crater Surtur II beside a tuft of* Bryum *sp. (e) The first mayweed,* Matricaria maritima *syn.* Tripleurospermum maritima, *in the sand-covered lava in quadrat S14. (f) A young angelic,* Angelica archangelica, *in quadrat L16. (Photos: S. Magnússon)*

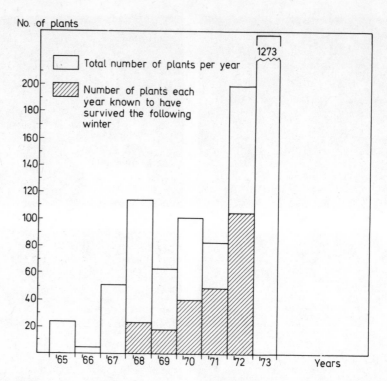

Figure 14.11. *A graph of the number of vascular plants growing on Surtsey 1965 to 1973 and the proportion which overwintered*

the tephra cone. This may to some extent explain the increased distribution of plants in the lava apron that took place in 1971.

During a detailed search for plants in the lava we came upon three small ferns that were growing down from a cave roof. These turned out to be small individuals of the bladder fern, *Cystopteris fragilis*, which is the most common fern in Iceland and grows both on the post-glacial lava as well as on other rocks and cliffs. The plants on Surtsey had reached two to three cm length when first observed and kept on developing, as they were sheltered and shaded from the direct sunlight (Figure 14.10d).

Until this time there had been an addition of approximately one new species of vascular plants to the island's flora every year since the colonisation of these plants started. However, in 1972, at least four new species were discovered. These were: *Angelica archangelica*, *Carex maritima*, a *Puccinellia* species, and *Matricaria maritima* syn. *Tripleurospermum maritimum*. All of these species are common on other islands in the Westman archipelago or on the lava flows of the mainland (Figure 14.10). The *Angelica* species was represented by two small seedlings with the cotyledons and seedwall attached. They were growing at the high-tide mark on the north-eastern part of the ness, which indicated that the plants developed from seed which had drifted to Surtsey on the ocean.

A small grass plant had been growing on the lava in quadrat M11 for some time. It was first incorrectly recorded in 1970 as a seedling of lyme-grass but was in 1972 definitely identified and listed as the sedge *Carex maritima*. The plant had not produced any flower stalks, but it had developed stolons and was by that time increasing vegetatively, so that several new individuals were being formed beside the mother plant.

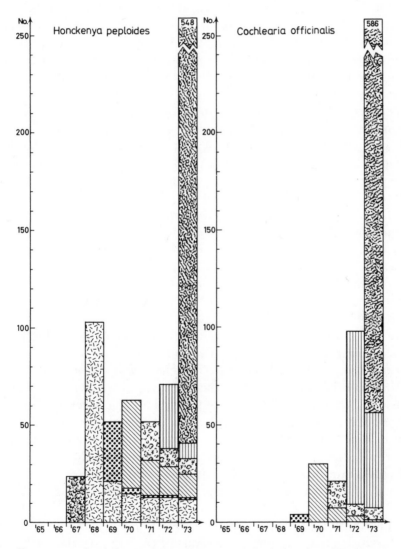

Figure 14.12. Graph showing the annual increase in individual numbers of Honckenya peploides *and* Cochlearia officinalis *on Surtsey. Columns of different shades show the new annual addition as well as the numbers of overwintering plants from previous years*

The third new species was the grass, *Puccinellia*, very likely of the species *maritima*, which is common on other islands and skerries in the neighbourhood. Two individuals representing this species were growing near one of the sites where a water container had been placed. This site, like the others where traps had been set up to catch fresh water micro-organisms, was frequently visited by birds. It is therefore very likely that these two plants also developed from seeds dispersed to the area by sea-gulls or other frequent bird visitors.

The fourth new species discovered in this year was the mayweed, *Matricaria maritima* syn. *Tripleurospermum maritimum*, a very common species on all the Westman Islands. The first plant of the species on Surtsey grew on the southern edge of the lava apron in a sand-covered hollow, which was also occupied by individuals of scurvy grass. It is likely that all the plants in the same hollow grew from seed brought to the edge of the lava rocks by birds, which often roost on these southern rocks or fly along the shore.

During the summer of 1971 there were 83 vascular plants on Surtsey, of which 49 individuals survived the winter 1971–72, or 59%. This was an even higher percentage of surviving individuals than the year before. The majority of the individuals that year were growing in the relatively secure sites of the lava, with fewer individuals on the northern ness than in previous years. This latter location is often overflooded during winter storms and is thus quite hazardous for the overwintering of plants. The corresponding percentages of overwintering plants for the previous winters are: 20% in 1968–69, 35% in 1969–70, and 53% in 1970–71, the graph Figure 14.11 shows the number of vascular plants growing on Surtsey during the years 1965 to 1973, as well as the number of overwintering plants for the last five years. It is obvious that each year an increased number of plants survive the winter. This must be due to the more secure location of growth and a steady increase of permanent members of plants (Table 14.6).

During the early years of colonisation *Honckenya peploides* was the most abundant plant on Surtsey, but in the summers of 1972 and 1973 the individuals of *Cochlearia officinalis* outnumbered all the other species. This is mostly due to the fertility of one plant, which produced a number of offsprings in both 1972 and 1973, and has formed a small colony of scurvy grass on the south shore. The graph in Figure 14.12, shows the annual increase in individual numbers of these two most frequent species of vascular plants on Surtsey, indicating also the proportion of overwintering plants every year.

The distribution of plants increased heavily in 1973. In 1972 there were 199 individuals discovered in 41 quadrats of the 234 quadrats covering the dryland on Surtsey. Five more quadrats were occupied by plants in 1972 than in the previous year. In 1973, the number of individual plants jumped

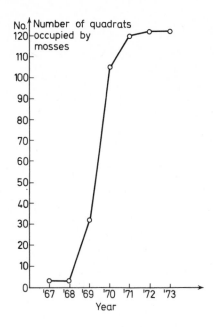

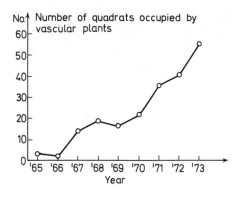

Figure 14.13. Graphs showing the number of quadrats occupied by vascular plants compared with those occupied by mosses during the period 1965 to 1973

to 1273, and these occupied 58 quadrats. The increased distribution of vascular plants on Surtsey can be shown by the number of quadrats the plants have occupied in the various years. The graph on Figure 14.13 shows that there has been a steady increase in the number of quadrats occupied during the last five years.

In Table 14.7 is a list of species of vascular plants found on Surtsey during the past nine years. It is noticeable that the first colonist, which was the sea rocket, *Cakile edentula*, has not become a permanent member of the plant colony. It is an annual plant and, although it has produced seed on the island,

Table 14.7. Total number of vascular plants annually found growing on Surtsey

Species	65	66	67	68	69	70	71	72	73
Cakile edentula	23	1	22		2			1	33
Elymus arenarius		4	4	6	5	4	3		66
Honckenya peploides			24	103	52	63	52	71	548
Mertensia maritima		1		4				15	25
Cochlearia officinalis					4	30	21	98	586
Stellaria media						4	2	2	1
Cystopteris fragilis							1	4	3
Angelica archangelica								2	2
Carex maritima								1	1
Puccinellia sp.								2	1
Matricaria maritima								1	5
Unidentified plants				1			4	2	1
Festuca rubra									1
Total	23	5	51	114	63	101	83	199	1273

Table 14.6. List of vascular plants on Surtsey which have lived for two years or longer, with their location and identification number

Species	Quadrat	Number	67	68	69	70	71	72	73
						Years of growth			
Carex maritima	M 11	70–72				x	x	x	x
Cochlearia officinalis	J 18	70–18				x	x		
— —	K 18	70–29				x	x		
— —	K 18	70–31				x	x	x	x
— —	L 17	70–10				x	x		
— —	L 17	70–12				x	x		
— —	N 13	71–70					x	x	x
— —	O 6	70–19				x	x	x	
— —	P 10	71–71					x	x	x
— —	P 17	71–57					x	x	x
— —	R 11	71–75					x	x	x
— —	S 14	70–74				x	x	x	x
— —	S 14	71–54					x	x	x
— —	S 14	71–55					x	x	x
— —	S 14	72–34						x	x
— —	S 14	72–37						x	x
— —	S 14	72–41						x	x
— —	S 14	72–42						x	x
— —	S 14	72–44						x	x
— —	S 14	72–45						x	x
— —	S 14	72–53						x	x
Cystopteris fragilis	I 8	72–113						x	x
— —	N 9						x	x	x
Elymus arenarius	F 15	67–23	x	x					
Honckenya peploides	D 12	70–37				x	x	x	x
— —	E 11	70–47				x	x		
— —	E 11	70–48				x	x	x	
— —	E 11	70–55				x	x		
— —	E 11	70–56				x	x	x	x
— —	E 11	72–99						x	x
— —	E 11	72–100						x	x
— —	E 12	68–48		x	x				
— —	E 12	68–?		x	x				
— —	E 12	69–42			x	x			
— —	E 12	70–35				x	x	x	x
— —	E 12	70–43				x	x	x	
— —	E 12	70–53				x	x	x	
— —	E 12	70–54				x	x	x	x
— —	E 13	68–?		x	x	x			
— —	E 13	69–62			x	x	x	x	x
— —	F 13	70–42				x	x	x	x
— —	F 13	70–60				x	x	x	x
— —	F 13	70–69				x	x		
— —	F 13	71–43					x	x	x
— —	F 13	71–45					x	x	x
— —	F 13	71–46					x	x	x
— —	F 13	71–47					x	x	x

Table 14.6 (continued)

Species		Quadrat	Number	Years of growth						
				67	68	69	70	71	72	73
Honckenya peploides		F 14	72–83						x	x
—	—	F 15	68–?		x	x				
—	—	G 13	70–39				x	x	x	x
—	—	G 16	68–102		x	x				
—	—	G 16	68–103		x	x				
—	—	I 4	71–35					x	x	x
—	—	I 4	71–68					x	x	x
—	—	I 4	72–114						x	x
—	—	I 18	68–63		x	x	x	x	x	x
—	—	I 18	71–67					x	x	
—	—	J 4	72–30						x	x
—	—	J 13	71–63					x	x	x
—	—	J 17	68–6		x	x	x	x	x	
—	—	J 17	68–24		x	x	x	x	x	x
—	—	J 17	70–25				x	x	x	x
—	—	J 18	68–3		x	x				
—	—	J 18	68–4		x	x	x	x	x	x
—	—	J 18	68–8		x	x	x	x	x	x
—	—	J 18	68–21		x	x	x	x	x	x
—	—	J 18	68–22		x	x	x	x	x	x
—	—	J 18	68–23		x	x	x	x	x	x
—	—	J 18	68–64		x	x	x	x	x	x
—	—	J 18	68–70		x	x	x	x	x	x
—	—	J 18	68–87		x	x	x	x	x	x
—	—	J 18	69–50			x	x			
—	—	J 18	70–4				x	x	x	x
—	—	J 18	70–20				x	x	x	x
—	—	J 18	70–30				x	x	x	
—	—	J 18	70–64				x	x	x	x
—	—	J 18	72–109						x	x
—	—	K 5	72–56						x	x
—	—	K 17	68–83		x	x	x	x	x	x
—	—	K 18	68–56		x	x	x	x	x	x
—	—	N 10	71–69					x	x	x
—	—	M 10	72–108						x	x
—	—	R 17	68–101		x	x	x			
—	—	R 17	68–?		x	x				
Puccinellia sp.		R 14	72–90						x	x
Stellaria media		R 14	71–115						x	x
Matricaria maritima		S 14	72–40						x	x

it has to rely on the annual seed maturity and seed supply to the island as well as on the growing conditions at the tide mark. The *Cochlearia officinalis* occupies a more secure location and develops seed earlier than the *Cakile*. Plants of *Honckenya peploides* are the most permanent colonisers. They are perennial and are gradually increasing in size and development of flowering branches.

The main location of the vascular plants during the summer of 1973 was, in general, the same as in previous years; east of the tephra cone, Strompfjall in quadrats J17 and J18, near the hut in quadrats E12 and E13, and in the Black Gully quadrats F13 and G13. The fourth location was on the northern ness, and the fifth site has been named the Light Hill, S14, on the southern part of the lava where a number of plants were found occupying an area of 80–100 sq. m.

The study of vascular plants has been performed in such a way that during every year continuous observations are made throughout the summer. As new individuals are found, their location and stage of growth is recorded and their progress of development followed during the summer. Every plant is then marked with a stake bearing a specific number. The positions of all plants are finally plotted on an aerial photograph. Every year these locations have then been drawn on a map of the island, which also bears the grid of checkers or quadrats identified numerically and alphabetically. The locations of all the higher plants found on the island from the beginning can thus be detected and are shown on the map series (Figure 14.5). On the same maps the total distribution of moss is also plotted.

By comparing the maps from year to year, it may be noted that the invasion of higher plants has mostly come towards the northern ness. The vegetation there has been unstable, and some seed have apparently been blown around the eastern side of Strompfjall and up towards the lava edge.

These plants enjoy a greater security than the individuals out on the ness, and the site is sheltered from the north wind. Except for the colony at Light Hill there is only a sporadic occupation of higher plants on the lava apron.

In contrast to the moss vegetation, which has mainly occupied the lava, the higher plants have largely settled on the sandy beach and gradually invaded the sand-filled hollows of the lava. There they have joined the moss in forming the juvenile community, which often only consists of one higher plant, a few moss species, an odd alga, moulds, and bacteria. Most of the individual plants, however, are still so far apart that one can hardly speak of a community, and there is only a slight relationship between the colonisation of moss and the vascular plants. They are dispersing to the island and occupying their habitats independently. The bacteria that have been found growing on the organic matter secreted by the plants are, however, obviously dependent on the latter.

THE TERRESTRIAL ANIMALS

So far there has not been a great deal of organic matter produced by the terrestrial vegetation on Surtsey, and the producers have thus not been able to support any substantial amount of life occupying higher tropic levels. Most of the animals observed on Surtsey are, therefore, visitors that obtain their energy from sources not directly belonging to the island's ecosystem. A few of the animals may be considered partial occupants, and some have reproduced on the island although their food is sought away from their breeding site. Still, a smaller number of individuals may be listed as permanent colonisers of Surtsey.

THE MICROFAUNA

In the surface tephra just above high-tide line marine algae are washed up with the ocean spray. There this organic matter is used as food by bacteria, fungi, and a few lower animals. In 1968 this substrate was sampled and an analysis performed to determine whether species of lower animals were present and to investigate their composition and abundance. The tephra samples were examined microscopically for amoebae, testacea, flagellates, and ciliates. This was performed after a 2–3 g portion of the tephra had been spread out on agar plates with different culture media and an addition of the bacterium, *Aerobacter*, which was used as a food source.

This examination revealed that only flagellated protozoa (Class Mastigophora) were present. The identified species were *Oikomonas termo* (Order Chrysomonadida), *Phalansterium solitarium*, *Sainouron mikroteron* (Order Protomonadida), and *Helkesimastix faeicola* (Order Rhizomastigida). The quantitative determination of the individuals showed that there were on the average only 290 flagellates in a gram of tephra, both mobile cells and cysts. This is a much lower number than would be found in the soil of a highly developed grassland community. These flagellated protozoa may be pioneer species of the Surtsey substrate. They can easily disperse to the island by wind, being carried on or with dust particles. They may be the first to appear, as these species have lighter spores than most other protozoa. Above the high-tide mark the organisms find their appropriate food source, and in this habitat they become the primary consumers in the ecosystem.

Higher up on the island, near fumaroles and other moist spots in the Surtur craters where algae and moss have gradually established their first colonies, the microfauna may find adequate food supply, and there the various airborne spores dispersing to the island have a fair chance of developing.

In 1970 some of these locations were visited and samples taken from patches of algae and moss growing in lava caves and on edges of fumaroles with moist surfaces formed by the condensed steam. After culturing the vegetation samples on nutrient media of a solid or liquid substrate, different microzoa were discovered. These were individuals belonging to the amoebae such as *Valkampfia*, *Naegleria*, and *Thecamaeba* species, and Testacea such as *Euglypha* species. Of the ciliates the species *Cyclidium citrullis* could be identified, as well as two species of bdelloid rotifers. All of these forms are considered to be cosmopolitans and capable of reproducing asexually. The animals are readily transformed into resting forms and can in this stage be transported to the island. These microzoa are all capable of withstanding severe environmental changes such as drought and frost. It is therefore clear that they are capable of being the pioneer consumers at the lower trophic level of the food chain in the moist lava habitat on Surtsey, where they feed on the blue–green algae, *Nostoc*, and bacteria.

It should also be pointed out that already in 1971 two nematodes; *Acrobeloides nanus* and a species of *Monhystera*, were discovered on the island, although these individuals were obtained from the rather artificial habitat of the fresh water container so often mentioned in previous chapters of this book. At least the former species is comparable to other animals so far observed in the microfauna of Surtsey with respect to reproduction, distribution, and the ability to withstand severe environmental conditions. The *A. nanus* nematode is a cosmopolitan species with a wide distribution in Europe. It is parthenogenetic and has the ability to survive desiccation, so that these individuals can, better than many other animals, endure drought and thus successfully manage to disperse to Surtsey. They are bacteria-feeders, and occupy a very low trophic level.

THE TERRESTRIAL INVERTEBRATES

The first specimen of terrestrial invertebrates was a diptera fly, later identified as that of *Diamesa zernyi*. I collected this fly on 14 May 1964 on the western shore during the first spring of the island's existence, only half a year after the island's formation. The following summer five more specimens of flies and midges were collected, as well as two species of moths and the mite *Thinoseius spinosus*. It was especially interesting to note that the mite was apparently living on some dead midges and the *Heleomyza borealis*, which is a common fly on neighbouring islands, was living on the carcass of a bird. Thus, a food chain was already established, from the carcass, to the mite, and ending in a mould that was found living on one of the mites.

In 1966 glue-traps were set up on the island to capture flies, and a systematic collection of terrestrial Arthropods commenced (Figure 14.14). During

(a)

(b)

Figure 14.14. (a) Collecting insects from the glue trap. (b) Looking for insects beside a fumarole

that year 22 species of insects were recorded and four species of Arachnoidea. Since then a number of new species of Arthropods are recorded every year that passes. In the year 1967 56 species of Insecta and seven species of Arachnoidea were collected and in 1968 there was an addition of eight new species. In the years 1969 and 1970 the number had increased to 112 species of Insecta and 24 of Arachnoidea.

This large number of Arthropods so far discovered on Surtsey does not imply that the animals have all started colonising the island. On the contrary,

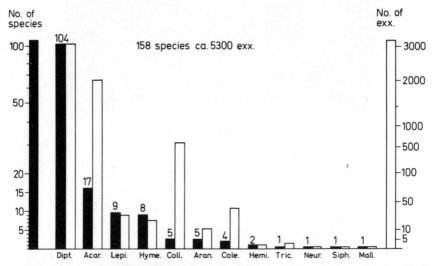

Figure 14.15. *Total number of terrestrial Arthropods found on Surtsey in 1970. Species—black, and specimens—white (Courtesy: C. H. Lindroth et al.)*

the majority of them are only casual visitors and very few may be considered permanent inhabitants.

The number of Arthropods already recorded on Surtsey may be considered high in relation to the total number known in Iceland. Out of the 850 species known to be established on the mainland, 158 have been collected on Surtsey, which indicates that the dispersal of insects to the island must be relatively easy (Figure 14.15).

As stated in the chapter on dispersal, there are several means of transport for the various terrestrial invertebrates; by own wing support, by wind, water, other animals, and man.

Many species of butterflies and moths have so far been recorded on Surtsey. In 1965 I found a specimen of *Autographa gamma*, which is not native to Iceland but migrates from the mainland of Europe, or from the British Isles. It and other Lepidoptera are excellent flyers and migrate over long distances on their own wing support.

All the insects discovered on Surtsey were winged, but it is doubtful that they could have managed to reach the island if they were not also aided by favourable winds. It has, for example, been noted that during strong northerly winds, 10–20 m/sec, the number of airborne individuals has increased markedly. Most of the 77 Diptera species are, as a result of this, considered to have reached Surtsey by these means of dispersal.

Ballooning of spiders is one way of dispersal which is aided by wind. In 1966 a small living spider of the family Linyphiidae was discovered on the northern ness of the island. This spider had apparently been ballooning on the long thread secreted by the animal, especially during the immature stage.

On a few occasions it has been possible to demonstrate that insects may be transported to Surtsey by sea. Such may have been the dispersal of the mite *Oribotritia faeroensis*, which was discovered on the island in 1966. The eleven individuals of this species were found alive on a gate-pole, which very likely had drifted to the island from the dumps on Heimaey. In a similar way the weevil, *Otiorrhynchus arcticus*, must have been carried to the island, as it is not able to fly. It is abundant on Heimaey and could have been transported by some kind of floats, but hardly by direct transport in the ocean, as experiments have shown that it does not survive immersion in water for more than 24 hours.

It was demonstrated during our bird collection that a number of birds were carrying insects on the exterior of their bodies, and even in their alimentary tracts, but some insects are also found to have mites, Acari, in their nymphal stage as parasites, and in that way have transported mites to the island.

Although there are strict regulations regarding the import of plants and animals to Surtsey, man has brought at least two flies, *Drosophila funebris* and *Musca domestica*, to the island. These two species were found inside the scientists' hut and were very likely transported with the provisions.

ORIGIN AND COLONISATION

The immigrating invertebrates so far collected on Surtsey have mostly derived from the other islands of the archipelago. The insect fauna of these islands was consequently investigated in 1968, so that it is now possible to determine which of the animals hitherto found on Surtsey could have derived from these islands and thus also the shortest possible distance of dispersal. Heimaey being the largest of the islands, also has the greatest number of invertebrate species and has, very likely, supplied Surtsey with a number of immigrants. It has also been demonstrated that some of the individuals found on Surtsey must have come from the mainland of Iceland, as no representatives of the same species are found on the Westman Islands. Some of the active flyers, such as the Noctuid moths and butterflies, must even have derived from Europe, as they are not native to Iceland. These individuals have therefore dispersed over the Atlantic with air-currents and finally landed on the island. It must be borne in mind that the greatest number of individuals belonging to the various species of terrestrial inverte-brates so far found on Surtsey are only casual visitors that happen to be carried to the island and have little chance of survival. Only a small number have been able to live for any length of time, and only a few of these have been able to breed and may be considered to have become temporary or permanent inhabitants. The main hindrance to a successful colonisation is the lack of available food supply for the animals in this new habitat, as the vegetation has, until recently, not produced any substantial amount of organic matter. The major food source has been the organic matter washed ashore from the sea. Insects that can breed and rear their offspring on such carcasses have therefore had the best chance to colonise. The three following species are all terrestrial invertebrates that have occupied the beach on Surtsey.

1. In 1965 the fly, *Heleomyza borealis*, was discovered and later found to be breeding abundantly in carcasses of fish and birds on the coast of Surtsey. Since then this fly has been breeding periodically on the island, but its sur-vival depends on the availability of food, and sea-gulls are hard competitors, devouring rapidly any carcasses washed upon the shore, so food is not permanently available.

2. The first collembola, *Archistoma besselsi*, was discovered on Surtsey in 1967. It spreads easily with the sea currents along the coast of Iceland and has apparently been dispersed on the ocean surface to Surtsey, where it has colonised the beach and become abundant and a permanent inhabitant.

3. In 1970 a chironomid midge, *Cricotopus variabilis*, was found breeding in shallow pools at the tidal zone on Surtsey. This midge is common on Heimaey and it is reasonable to assume that it has become a permanent resident on Surtsey.

All these individuals are finding enough food source on the beach and are capable of surviving and reproducing in the coastal habitat of the island, but farther inland no invertebrates have yet had a chance to colonise.

THE BIRDS

Sea-gulls were among the first living creatures to set foot on Surtsey, and they have continued to soar about its beaches, or roost on its hills and cliffs ever since. The ocean around the Westman Islands is extremely rich in marine life used by various birds as a source of food. Sea-gulls and waders feed on carcasses of marine animals cast ashore on the island, or make their catch from the ocean farther out and sometimes bring their prey on to dry land to devour it there. The remnants of such carcasses may, in turn, serve as an energy source for lower forms of life. The presence of sea-gulls on the island also greatly affects the future soil of Surtsey by their excreta supplying fertiliser, containing both minerals and organic matter. This is mainly deposited along the edge of the cliffs of the southern coast, on the sandy beach of the northern ness and on high peaks of the tephra cones. As previously mentioned, the birds have played their part in transporting diaspores of plants to Surtsey and are even carriers of various invertebrates. The birds are therefore very important members of the island's ecosystem, but until the present time they have mostly had to rely upon an energy source obtained from outside the boundaries of the island.

From the very beginning of the Surtsey research various observations were performed with regard to birds visiting the island. Records have been made, by skilled bird-watchers, of birds seen since the formation of the island. And during certain periods in early spring and autumn, birds have been collected for closer examination by ornithologists. In the spring migratory birds fly north from the continent of Europe and the British Isles, frequently visiting Surtsey, which is the first possible landing place for a number of these birds after crossing the Atlantic. In the autumn the birds have a reverse route when flying south from Greenland or the mainland of Iceland, and they may have a short visit to Surtsey. During such a visit the birds sometimes empty their guts and deposit seed with their excreta. I have witnessed a flock of geese in flight over the island, bombing it with their droppings as they became disturbed by the presence of man on the island.

During the autumn, Iceland is often visited by drift migrants from northern Europe or Siberia that are making their journey south by the west coast of Europe and drift off their course over the Atlantic. Many of such stragglers that have been seen or caught on Surtsey may also be carriers of seeds, which are abundantly available at this time of the year. The ornithological work on Surtsey has been important in demonstrating the exact time of arrival of the various migrants to Iceland, their physical condition after their flight across the ocean, the part they may play in transporting other organisms, as well as their exodus in the autumn.

Of the 230 species recorded as seen in Iceland, 60 have so far visited Surtsey. Following the first visit of the sea-gulls a group of redwings, *Tardus iliacus*, were seen in the early spring of 1964. In May of the same year I observed a snow bunting, *Plectrophenax nivalis*, up on the lava and a few dunlins, *Calidris alpina*, and oystercatchers, *Haemotopus ostralegus*, feeding

(a)

Figure 14.16. The kittiwake,
Rissa tridactyla, is one of the
most common birds on Surtsey.
(a) Perching on the southern cliff
(Photo: S. Magnússon). (b) Young
birds on the lava (Photo:
E. Olafsson), (c) Mature birds
roosting on a ledge spotted with
guano (Photo: S. Magnússon)

(b)

(c)

on the Euphausids that had been washed ashore on the northern side of the island. The birds most frequently seen, however, were the sea-gulls, such as *Larus* and *Rissa* sp. The kittiwakes, *Rissa tridactyla*, may have been the first of the sea-gulls to alight on the island during intervals between eruptions, and in 1964 a flock of these birds frequently rested on the tephra bluffs on the northern side, or on vertical cliffs of lava that had been formed on the southern side of the island (Figure 14.16).

The great black-backed gull, *Larus marinus*, occupied the flat sandy beach and was accompanied by the herring gull, *Larus argentatus*, and the glaucous gull, *Larus hyperboreus*, in varying numbers during the first summer, as well as the arctic tern, *Sterna paradisaea*. In early August a large flock of red-necked phalaropes, *Phalaropus lobatus*, was swimming close to the shore and later in the autumn an oiled specimen of a common guillemot, *Uria aalge*, was encountered. A single turtle dove, *Streptopelia turtur*, was seen on the lava flow on the south-western part of the island in October. This last species occasionally drifts off course and could be one of the best carriers of seeds, if it flew with a full crop to the island.

In 1965 a pair of ravens, *Corvus corax*, occasionally visited the island and was seen there frequently in the following years. During that summer four additional species of birds were recorded.

In 1966 23 species were recorded as seen on the island, among which was a merlin, *Falco columbarius*, that flew over the lava in search of prey, which may have been the wheatear, *Oenanthe oenanthe*, seen during the same period. as well as a few other passerines. A merlin had been seen eating a wheatear on Surtsey, and later several carcasses of wheatears and meadow pipits, *Anthus pratensis*, were observed. These birds, in turn, may have been feeding on insects that obtained their energy source from a still lower trophic level.

In 1967 there were 29 species of migratory birds observed on or around Surtsey, besides the 13 species of resident sea-birds that frequently occupy the neighbouring islands. Among these were redshanks, *Tringa totanus*, and golden plovers, *Pluvialis apricaria*, in addition to several species of geese such as the greylags, *Anser anser*, pinkfeet, *Anser brachyrhynchus*, and a number of barnacle geese, *Branta leucopsis*, that either flew over the island or settled on the plains of the northern ness. One long-eared owl, *Asio otus*, was caught in the lava that spring, where it was apparently seeking some prey. This was available in abundance among the exhausted passerine migrants such as the white wagtail, *Motacilla alba*, which was frequently seen catching flies around the scientists' hut.

The following year (1968) a whooper swan, *Cygnus musicus*, visited the island, as well as several ducks; mallards, *Anas platyrhynchos*, teals, *Anas crecca*, widgeons, *Anas penelope*, and the red-breasted merganser, *Mergus serrator*.

Among birds collected or observed in 1969 was a squacco heron, *Ardeola ralloides*. This bird was new to Iceland. Such a discovery could be expected, as Surtsey is situated farther south than any other part of Iceland and the stragglers are most common on the southern shores of Iceland in the autumn. During this same summer nine other drifting migrants were encountered. Among them was a short-eared owl, *Asio flammeus*, a European robin, *Erithacus rubecula*, and a jackdove, *Corvus monedula*.

In the year 1970 a number of new visitors were spotted on the island such as: corncrake, *Crex crex*, a willow warbler, *Phylloscopus trochilus*, and a redstart, *Phoenicurus phoenicurus*, and with every passing year the number of bird species seen on the island increases.

Most of the drifting migrants are only unusual rarities that do not play any major role in the island's ecosystem. The major influence is without doubt exerted by the local sea-birds and the great populations of migrants that fly across the island regularly every spring and autumn.

Migratory birds coming from Iceland may fly over Surtsey in a southerly direction towards the British Isles, where they winter, or they may proceed to France, to the Iberian peninsula or all the way to West Africa. In the spring the route is reversed: the migrating birds head north and start arriving in Iceland in April. Much information pertaining to migration routes has been accumulated by using bird ringing, but thorough studies on the time of arrival and exodus of these birds by direct observation methods had not been practised in Iceland to any extent until the research began on Surtsey.

As Surtsey lay in the path of the migrating birds, it was considered to fulfil requirements for such a study. The island was therefore manned by experienced bird-watchers, both in spring and autumn, from the year 1967 to 1970. They observed the migration of birds and kept records of all birds seen on the island and in its vicinity. The main stream of migrants arrives at the south-eastern part of Iceland, leaving Surtsey somewhat off the direct route. During side-winds arriving birds may, however, in some years drift in great numbers to the island.

The redwing and the golden plover are early arrivers and are followed after mid-April by various waders, such as redshanks, *Tringa totanus*, or turn-stones, *Arenaria interpres*, which were often seen in hundreds during their stop-overs on Surtsey. In late April and the first days of May geese and various small passerines may visit the island in large numbers (Figure 14.17).

During the migration studies 100 to 200 individuals of 10 to 20 bird species were collected each year.

The smaller passerines had obviously sometimes barely made the journey across the Atlantic due to unfavourable winds, and landed quite exhausted on Surtsey. This could be observed by the general appearance of the birds and demonstrated by measuring the lack of fat deposits which

Figure 14.17. (a) A flock of kittiwakes, Rissa tridactyla, *on the northern ness. (b) A purple sandpiper,* Calidris maritima, *on the young lava. (c) A turnstone,* Arenaria interpres, *on the new sandy shore. (d) A group of red-necked phalaropes,* Phalaropus lobatus, *by the shoreline. (e) Arctic terns,* Sterna paradisaea, *resting on the island. (f) A young gannet,* Sula bassana, *by the newly rounded boulders (Photos: (a), (b), (c), (e), and (f) E. Olafsson; (d) S. Magnússon)*

(a)　*(b)*

(c)

Figure 14.18. *The fulmar,* Fulmarus glacialis, *is now nesting on Surtsey. (a) and (b) One of the first eggs being hatched. (c) The young and the mature bird by the nest (Photos: S. Magnússon)*

birds use on their oversea crossings. Such conditions were especially apparent in the case of wheatears that apparently sometimes proceed with a continuous migration flight from West Africa to Iceland. The ornithological work on Surtsey, furthermore, consisted in weighing and sexing the collected birds, as well as searching closely for any seeds that the birds might be carrying in their alimentary tract.

The greatest ornithological event, however, took place in the summer of 1970, when the first birds started nesting. These were sea-birds of species common to the Westman Islands, i.e. the fulmar, *Fulmarus glacialis*, and the black guillemot, *Cepphus grylle*. The former had built a nest on a ledge 10 m above sea-level in the cliffs on the western side of the island (Figure 14.18), whereas the latter had built its nest in a crevice in the lava rock on the south-west side. Both nests were successful and birds of both species have since successfully nested every year on the island. In 1971 the colonisation of birds proceeded with 10 to 11 fulmar nests and 6 black guillemot nests. In 1972 there were 13 fulmar nests and possibly 6 to 8 black guillemot nests dispersed along the rocks of the south-west coast. Both of these bird species are now breeding permanently on the island, with their colonies becoming an integral part of the island's ecosystem, although they have to obtain their food and feed their young from the nearby ocean.

The lack of food sources from the producers or primary consumers of the ecosystem still hinders colonisation of landbirds to any extent, and the nesting of such birds will hardly begin to take place in the near future, except by birds such as the raven that can make use of carcasses drifting ashore on Surtsey. The population of birds that may be considered permanent on the island is still small in numbers, but as the birds have colonised the island most divisions of the plant and animal kingdom have been represented on Surtsey. Now it is only a matter of time before the colonists develop further their new community.

THE VEGETATION OF THE ADJACENT LAND MASSES

One of the factors affecting colonisation of terrestrial plants on Surtsey is the available sources of species on the adjacent land masses.

As a background for evaluating the colonisation of plants on the new island, a good knowledge of the flora of these land masses is necessary. In the manual of vascular plants of Iceland records are made of some species of vascular plants growing in the Westman Islands as well as the various locations on the adjacent mainland. In order to establish better knowledge of the flora in this area, however, it was considered necessary for the Surtsey studies to carry out an investigation of the vegetation of these areas. They fall into three groups: 1. The outer Westman Islands; 2. Heimaey; and 3. The southern coast of Iceland.

REFERENCES

The bacteria and moulds

BROCK, T. D., 'Microbial life on Surtsey', *Surtsey Res. Progr. Rep.*, **2**, 9–13 (1966)
BROCK, T. D. and BROCK, M. L., 'Progress report on microbiological studies on Surtsey and the Icelandic mainland', *Surtsey Res. Progr. Rep.*, **3**, 6–12 (1967)
BROCK, T. D., 'Microbiological observations on Surtsey 1970', *Surtsey Res. Progr. Rep.*, **6**, 11–14 (1972)
KOLBEINSSON, A. and FRIDRIKSSON, S., 'Studies of micro-organisms on Surtsey, 1965–1966', *Surtsey Research Conference, Proceedings*, Reykjavik, 37–44 (1967)

KOLBEINSSON, A. and FRIDRIKSSON, S., 'A preliminary report on studies of micro-organisms on Surtsey', *Surtsey Res. Progr. Rep.*, **3**, 57–58 (1967)

KOLBEINSSON, A. and FRIDRIKSSON, S., 'Report on studies of micro-organisms on Surtsey, 1967', *Surtsey Res. Progr. Rep.*, **4**, 75–76 (1968)

PONNAMPERUMA, C., YOUNG, R. S. and CAREN, L. D., 'Some chemical and microbiological studies of Surtsey', *Surtsey Res. Progr. Rep.*, **3**, 70–80 (1967)

SCHWARTZ, W. and SCHWARTZ, A., 'Microbial activity on Surtsey', *Surtsey Res. Progr. Rep.*, **6**, 90–91 (1972)

SCHWARTZ, W. and SCHWARTZ, A., 'Geomikrobiologische Untersuchungen', *Zeitschrift für Allg. Mikrobiologie*, **12**, 287–300 (1972)

The algae

CASTENHOLZ, R. W., 'The occurrence of the thermophilic blue–green algae, *Mastigocladus laminosus*, on Surtsey in 1970', *Surtsey Res. Progr. Rep.*, **6**, 14–20 (1972)

BEHRE, K. and SCHWABE, G. H., 'Algenbefunde in den Kraterräumen auf Surtsey, Island, Sommer 1968', *Vorläufinge Mitteilung aus dem Max-Planck-Institut für Limnologie*, Plön (1969)

BEHRE, K. and SCHWABE, G. H., 'Auf Surtsey, Island im Sommer 1968 nachgewiesene nicht marine Algen', *Schr. Naturw. Ver. Schlesw.-Holst., Sonderband*, 31–100 (1970)

HENRIKSSON, E., HENRIKSSON, L. E. and PEJLER, B., 'Nitrogen fixation by blue–green algae on the island of Surtsey, Iceland', *Surtsey Res. Progr. Rep.*, **6**, 66–69 (1972)

SCHWABE, G. H. 'On the algae settlement in craters on Surtsey during Summer 1968', *Surtsey Res. Progr. Rep.*, **5**, 68–70 (1970)

SCHWABE, G. H., 'Pioniere der Besiedlung auf Surtsey', Umschau in *Wissenschaft und Technik*, 51–52 (1969)

SCHWABE, G. H., 'Blaualgen und Vorstufen der Bodenbildung auf vulkanischem Substrat, Bisherige Befunde auf Surtsey, Island', *Mitt. Dtsch. Bodenkundl. Ges.*, **10**, 198–199 (1970)

SCHWABE, G. H., 'Blue–green algae as pioneers on postvolcanic substrate, Surtsey, Iceland', *Proc. Ist. Internat. Symp. on Taxonomy and Biology of Blue–green Algae*, Madras (1970)

SCHWABE, G. H., 'Zur Ökogenese auf Surtsey', *Schr. Naturw. Ver. Schlesw.-Holst., Sonderband*, 101–120 (1970)

SCHWABE, G. H., 'Surtsey', *Kosmos*, **67**, 489–497 (1971)

SCHWABE, G. H., 'Die Ökogenese im terrestrichen Bereich postvulkanischer Substrate, Schematische Öbersicht bisheriger Befunde auf Surtsey, Island', *Peterm. Geograph. Mitt*, **4**, 168–173 (1971)

SCHWABE, G. H. and BEHRE, K., 'On the colonisation of the volcanic island Surtsey', *Schweiz. Zeitschr. Hydrol.*, **32**, 32–487 (1970)

SCHWABE, G. H. and BEHRE, K., 'Ökogenese der Insel Surtsey 1968–1970', *Naturwiss. Resch.*, **24**, 513–519 (1971)

SCHWABE, G. H. and BEHRE, K., 'Algae on Surtsey in 1969–1970', *Surtsey Res. Progr. Rep.*, **6**, 85–90 (1972)

The freshwater biota

MAGUIRE, B., jr., 'The early development of freshwater biota on Surtsey', *Surtsey Res. Progr. Rep.*, **4**, 83–88 (1968)

MAGUIRE, B., jr., 'Surtsey's freshwater biota after 14 months', *Surtsey Res. Progr. Rep.*, **5**, 63–68 (1970)

The lichens

KRISTINSSON, H., 'New plant species colonise Surtsey', *Náttúrufr.*, **37**, 105–111 (1968)

KRISTINSSON, H., 'Invasion of terrestrial plants on the new volcanic island Surtsey, Ecology and reclamation of devastated land', *Proc. Internat. Symp. Pennsylvania State Univ.*, London, 253–270 (1969)

KRISTINSSON, H., 'Flechtenbesiedlung auf Surtsey', *Schr. Naturw. Ver. Schlesw.-Holst.*, Sonderband, 29–30 (1970)

KRISTINSSON, H., 'Report on lichenological work on Surtsey and in Iceland', *Surtsey Res. Progr. Rep.*, **5**, 52–53 (1970)

KRISTINSSON, H., 'Studies on lichen colonisation in Surtsey 1970', *Surtsey Res. Progr. Rep.*, **6**, 77–78 (1972)

KRISTINSSON, H., 'Lichen colonisation in Surtsey 1971–73' (in print)

The mosses

BJARNASON, A. H. and FRIDRIKSSON, S., 'Moss on Surtsey, Summer 1969', *Surtsey Res. Progr. Rep.*, **6**, 9–11 (1972)

JÓHANNSSON, B., 'Bryological observation on Surtsey', *Surtsey Res. Progr. Rep.*, **4**, 61 (1968)

The vascular plants

EINARSSON, E., 'The colonisation of Surtsey, the new volcanic island by vascular plants, Aquilo, Ser. Botanica', **6**, *Societas Amicorum Naturae Ouluensis*, 172–182 (1967)

EINARSSON, E., 'Comparative ecology of colonising species of vascular plants', *Surtsey Res. Progr. Rep.*, **3**, 13–16 (1967)

EINARSSON, E., 'Comparative ecology of colonising species of vascular plants', *Surtsey Res. Progr. Rep.*, **4**, 9–21 (1968)

FRIDRIKSSON, S., 'The first species of higher plants in Surtsey, the new volcanic island', *Náttúrufr.*, **35**, 97–102 (1965)

FRIDRIKSSON, S., 'The pioneer species of vascular plants in Surtsey *Cakile edentula*', *Surtsey Res. Progr. Rep.*, **2**, 63–65 (1966)

FRIDRIKSSON, S., A second species of vascular plants discovered in Surtsey', *Surtsey Res. Progr. Rep.*, **3**, 17–19 (1967); also *Náttúrufr.*, **36**, 157–158 (1966)

FRIDRIKSSON, S., BJARNASON, A. H. and SVEINBJÖRNSSON, B., 'Vascular plants in Surtsey 1969', *Surtsey Res. Progr. Rep.*, **6**, 30–34 (1972)

FRIDRIKSSON, S., SVEINBJÖRNSSON, B. and MAGNÚSSON, S., 'Vegetation on Surtsey summer 1970', *Surtsey Res. Progr. Rep.*, **6**, 54–60 (1972)

The microfauna

HOLMBERG, O. and PEJLER, B., 'On the terrestrial microfauna of Surtsey during the summer 1970', *Surtsey Res. Progr. Rep.*, **6**, 69–73 (1972)

SMITH, H. G., 'An analysis of Surtsey substratum for Protozoa', *Surtsey Res. Progr. Rep.*, **5**, 78–80 (1970)

The terrestrial invertebrates

LINDROTH, C. H., ANDERSON, N. and BÖDVARSSON, H., 'Report on the Surtsey investigation in 1965, Terrestrial invertebrates', *Surtsey Res. Progr. Rep.*, **2**, 15–17 (1966)

LINDROTH, C. H., 'Terrestrial invertebrates', *Surtsey Research Conference, Proceedings,* Reykjavik, 36 (1967)

LINDROTH, C. H., 'Djurvärlden erövrar en ny ö, Surtsey vid Island', *Naturens Verden,* 244–252 (1967)

LINDROTH, C. H., ANDERSSON, H., BÖDVARSSON, H. and RICHTER, S. H., 'Report on the Surtsey investigation in 1966, terrestrial invertebrates', *Surtsey Res. Progr. Rep.,* **3**, 59–67 (1967)

LINDROTH, C. H., ANDERSSON, H., BÖDVARSSON, H. and RICHTER, S. H., 'Preliminary report on the Surtsey investigation in 1967, terrestrial invertebrates', *Surtsey Res. Progr. Rep.,* **4**, 78–82 (1968)

LINDROTH, C. H., ANDERSSON, H., BÖDVARSSON, H. and RICHTER, S. H., 'Preliminary report on the Surtsey investigation in 1968, terrestrial invertebrates', *Surtsey Res. Progr. Rep.,* **5**, 53–60 (1970)

LINDROTH, C. H., ANDERSSON, H., BÖDVARSSON, H., PEJLER, B. and RICHTER, S. H., 'Preliminary report on the Surtsey investigation in 1969 and 1970, terrestrial invertebrates', *Surtsey Res. Progr. Rep.,* **6**, 78–82 (1972)

LINDROTH, C. H., ANDERSSON, H., BÖDVARSSON, H. and RICHTER, S., 'Surtsey, Iceland. Supplementum', **5**, *Entomologica Scandinavica*, Munksgaard, Copenhagen, 280 (1973)

SOHLENIUS, B., 'Nematodes from Surtsey', *Surtsey Res. Progr. Rep.,* **6**, 97–99 (1972)

The birds

GUDMUNDSSON, F., 'Birds observed on Surtsey', *Surtsey Res. Progr. Rep.,* **2**, 23–28 (1966)

GUDMUNDSSON, F., 'Bird observation on Surtsey in 1966', *Surtsey Res. Progr. Rep.,* **3**, 37–41 (1967)

GUDMUNDSSON, F., 'Ornithological works on Surtsey in 1967', *Surtsey Res. Progr. Rep.,* **4**, 51–55 (1968)

GUDMUNDSSON, F., 'Bird migration studies on Surtsey in the spring of 1968', *Surtsey Res. Progr. Rep.,* **5**, 30–39 (1970)

GUDMUNDSSON, F., 'Ornithological works on Surtsey in 1969 and 1970', *Surtsey Res. Progr. Rep.,* **6**, 64–66 (1972)

15

THE OUTER WESTMAN ISLANDS

TOPOGRAPHICAL FEATURES

According to present knowledge, geologists believe the Westman Islands to have been created by volcanic activities towards the end of and after the last glaciation. The formation of Surtsey has clarified facts concerning the origin of other islands in the group lying along a NE.–SW. tectonic fissure, which is a part of the Atlantic ridge. Remnants of volcanic craters are noticeable throughout the islands, which are mostly made of palagonite tuff, consolidated volcanic ash, with streaks and veins of intruded basalt. The palagonite tuff accounts for most of the bedrock, but large areas of Heimaey are like Surtsey also covered with lava (Figure 15.1). These two are the largest islands, and they show greater variation in topography than the smaller members of the group, some of which are mere stacks, 50 m high with a mantle of vegetation on the slanting summit. The soil in the older islands is rather deep, loessy in character, fertile and rich in organic matter due to bird-droppings. Sea-birds inhabit the islands in great numbers; among these is the puffin, *Fratercula arctica*, which digs deep nesting holes in the soil on the top of the islands, whereas the various other sea-bird species inhabit the cliffs (Figure 15.2).

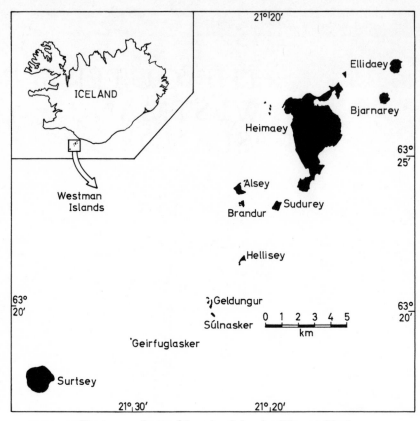

Figure 15.1. A map of Surtsey and the other Westman Islands

Tuff   Loam   Turf

Figure 15.2. A cross section of puffin ground from Súlnasker. The puffin, Fratercula arctica, excavates a burrow in the loamy soil which may be one metre thick on top of the tuff bedrock. In between the entrances to the nesting holes are tussocks of red fescue, Festuca rubra, growing on a dense carpet of turf. The fescue tufts often hang over the opening, hiding the entrance to the hole. The fulmar, Fulmarus glacialis, nests on the ledges.

METHOD OF RESEARCH

In the summer of 1965, botanical investigations were made of the vegetation of all these outer islands, as well as on three mountain isolates in southern Iceland. Herbarium material as well as live specimens were collected for laboratory study. During the summer of 1966, an examination of the vegetation of individual islands was continued, with a detailed study of the number of species, their distribution and associations. Emphasis was placed on the ecological studies. Plant distribution was measured by two methods. Most frequently the point-measurement method was used for the estimation of coverage of species as given in percentage terms. Further measurements were also undertaken with a special view to comparison with observations made previously in 1933 on Bjarnarey and Heimaey.

THE PLANT COMMUNITIES

The vegetation of the outer islands can be classified into four plant communities: the dry meadowland, the puffin-ground vegetation, the coastal cliff vegetation and the angelica cluster.

I. The dry meadowland vegetation has a wide distribution, predominating on the northern islands, and being the second largest plant association on the southern islands. It is situated on the level or sloping summits where the soil is dry and shallow. The soil of the dry meadowland is rich in organic matter due to the high annual productivity of this community and its low decomposition. A layer of turf is thus formed at the top. On the southern-most island this top layer includes some fresh volcanic ash derived from the Surtsey eruption. The thickness of the ash varies in proportion to the distance from its source of origin. On the island of Álsey 14 km distant from Surtsey the ash layer was 2–3 cm thick. Below the turf layer the soil is rich in minerals, which derive from the basic tuff below. The meadowland is to some extent fertilised by various sea-birds constantly swarming over the islands during the nesting period. This accounts for a rather high fertility level of the soil and vigorous growth. The dry meadowland has a predominance of grasses, with *Festuca rubra*, *Poa pratensis* and *Agrostis tenuis* as the dominant species. The associated species are *Ranunculus acris*, *Poa trivialis*, *Rumex acetosa*, *Cerastium caespitosum* and *Taraxacum acromauris*. All these species are of common occurrence in cultivated hayfields in Iceland. As a rule, the meadowland vegetation on the outer islands resembles some cultivated grasslands as regards species and growing conditions. The Bryophyta are completely absent from this plant community, as is the case with well-cultivated hayfields. The growth of the grass species is vigorous. The height of mature culms reaches 50 cm and the yield is five to six tons D.M. per hectare, judged from samples collected in Sudurey and Álsey. The productivity is thus quite high, almost comparable with that of an average cultivated hayfield in Iceland. When this observation was made, no sheep had been grazing on the southern islands since the volcanic activity started in the Surtsey area. Previous to that a number of sheep had been out to pasture on the island all the year round as far back as records go. The grazing of the sheep may be selective to some extent; in dry seasons the sheep have a tendency to feed on the more succulent broad-leaved herbs, as drinking water is limited. It is the farmers' opinion that the vegetation on the islands became more productive after the volcanic activity commenced and that *Matricaria* and *Ranunculus* are now more abundant. The volcanic activity may have directly affected the growth by the fertilising effect of the ash or indirectly by terminating the grazing of sheep.

II. The puffin ground can be regarded as a derivative of meadowland, as the puffin hardly establishes nesting colonies except in grass-covered soil. On some of the islands genuine meadowland is hardly to be found, as it is occupied and deformed by the presence of the puffin. This association forms the bulk of the vegetation on the southern islands, and is usually situated on slopes facing the sea where the puffin, *Fratercula arctica*, nests in deep holes. There are approximately three to four nesting holes per square metre. The three main species of vascular plants growing there are: *Festuca rubra*, *Matricaria maritima* and *Stellaria media*. The *Festuca* predominates with an approximate cover of 70%, while *Matricaria* and *Stellaria* are the associated species. The soil is deep and damp with a high content of organic matter. The fertility level of the soil is extremely high as a result of bird droppings. These high fertility conditions are quite selective, presumably favouring the red fescue rather than other grass species. At this level the fescue remains highly vegetative and has a high ratio of leaves to culms. The puffin-ground vegetation has an intense bluish–green tint, contrasting with the bleaker tint of the dry meadowland. This difference becomes more conspicuous towards autumn, as the grass in the dry meadowland reaches maturity and becomes higher in fibre content and wilts earlier than in the puffin ground. The soil is broken up by the puffin into small columns with tufts of red fescue covering the network of tunnels and trenches. Thus, this honeycomb-structure of soil appears to be a continuous mat of vegetation. However, where there is a break in the fescue cover, the associated species have a chance to establish themselves.

Whenever the breeding grounds of puffin are densely populated, the growth of the red fescue is hampered by the excavation of the birds. On these occasions, the associated species are favoured, sometimes even allowing the *Matricaria* to predominate, but in rare instances *Cochlearia* and *Atriplex* occupy the space. Apparently this high fertility level, the special water retention of the turf soil, as well as the intense aeration caused by the digging, play an important role in this selective habitat. The soils differ in the extent of aeration from other highly fertile soils in Iceland, such as those of hayfields in the neighbourhood of stables and farmhouses. In that case *Poa annua* dominates, but this species is hardly present in the vegetation of the puffin colony, except in one instance, i.e. on the island of Súlnasker, where it was found growing on the edge of a small basin containing rain-water.

III. The coastal cliff vegetation is situated in the splashing zone, forming a fringe round the islands. This is, however, not necessarily continuous. It is the vegetation of the slanting slope, but is interrupted wherever the cliffs are too steep to hold this type of vegetation. Its lower margin is at high-tide mark and the upper border is contiguous with the puffin ground. This zone varies in width, reaching a higher level on the southern side, which is exposed to the Atlantic where the surf is more intense, than on the side facing the mainland. This vegetation does not form a continuous mat. It is an open community with plants growing in small patches in depressions and crevices, where some soil or anchorage is to be found on the otherwise bare rock. Estimated ground-coverage is 1–5% of the total area. The predominating species are *Puccinellia maritima* and *Cochlearia officinalis* with *Armeria vulgaris*, *Atriplex patula* and *Plantago maritima* as associated species.

IV. The angelica cluster is situated on slopes or rocky shelves on the northern sides of some of the islands. The dominant species is *Angelica archangelica*, with *Matricaria maritima* and *Stellaria media* as associated species. On the margins of the cluster these are sometimes also accompanied by *Festuca rubra*. An account will now be given of the plant communities of the outer islands, beginning with the largest island and ending with the smallest, the communities being grouped in the four associations.

ELLIDAEY

Ellidaey, which has an area of about 0.46 sq km, is somewhat low-lying, but slopes steeply to the sea. In the centre of the island there is a sizeable crater, Bunki, which is covered with vegetation, and on either side of it there are small level spaces or hollows. Dry meadowland predominates on the island, with a puffin ground on the seaward slopes. The dominant species of the meadowland of Ellidaey was *Agrostis tenuis*, average 62%, with associated species *Festuca rubra* 26% and *Poa pratensis* 12%. *Stellaria media* was also present, though it did not occur in the measurements. In the puffin ground the dominant species was *Festuca rubra* 74%, with associated species *Stellaria media* 19.5% and *Poa pratensis* 5%. Bare patches were 1.5%. In one measurement taken up on the crater rim, on the outskirts of a puffin colony, *Poa pratensis* was the dominant species with 45% ground cover. The major associated species were *Stellaria media* 30%, *Festuca rubra* 15% and *Agrostis tenuis* 7.5%. This was a marginal strip between puffin ground and dry meadowland proper. These strips occur frequently. On Ellidaey, only 23 species of vascular plants have been found, which is a rather low number in relation to the size of the island. No moist spots occur on this island, and this excludes some species that grow on other islands where such conditions occur. Ellidaey is the only one of the outer islands still used for grazing sheep, though most of the islands having enough vegetation were formerly used for this purpose.

BJARNAREY

Bjarnarey is the second largest of the outer islands, excluding Surtsey, with nearly 0.32 sq. km, and is the highest, about 164 m, surrounded by cliffs on all sides except the north-east, where landing is easiest. In the centre of the island there is a grass-grown crater with a bowl-shaped depression at its summit. Round it there is some level ground, but otherwise slopes that descend right to the cliff's edge. Dry meadowland dominates on the island, but there is also a substantial area clothed with puffin-ground vegetation on the slopes. Coastal cliff vegetation occurs only at the above-mentioned landing-place, with sparse growths of *Puccinellia* and *Cochlearia*. On the Angelica Shelf 'Hvannhilla' there is an area of angelica cluster.

The flora of Bjarnarey is the richest in plant species of the outer islands. Of vascular plants 30 species have been found on this island, five not occurring on the other islands: *Anthoxanthum odoratum*, *Galium verum*, *Luzula multiflora*, *Potentilla anserina* and *Equisetum arvense*. These all grow in a relatively small area of dry meadowland on the south side of the crater, a place well sheltered from salt water spray, which might inhibit their distribution elsewhere. The dominant species of the dry meadowland were *Agrostis tenuis*, with about 40% coverage, *Festuca rubra* 37%, and *Poa pratensis* 20% on the average. Associated species covered 3%. *Agrostis tenuis* appeared to increase in frequency with increased distance from the puffin ground, being most abundant where the soil was poorest, which agrees with observations on Ellidaey. A comparison of the 1966 measurements with those made in 1933 shows that there has been little change in the composition of associations during the period. It appears, however, that there has been one change in the dry meadowland, inasmuch as *Cerastium* and *Euphrasia* have almost disappeared and been replaced by *Anthoxanthum*. This latter species may have been present before, though not occurring in the 1933 measurements owing to its limited extent. *Stellaria* which was observed in 1933 is, however, still present, though not occurring in the present measurements of the area. This change in the flora can also be explained by the fact that annual species are generally subject to substantial fluctuations from one year to the next. There is a large puffin ground on Bjarnarey. The dominant species are *Festuca rubra* with about 58% coverage, associated species *Stellaria media* with 20% coverage, and *Poa pratensis* with 11% coverage. The *Poa* is found especially on the fringes of the puffin ground, forming there a kind of marginal strip, as on Ellidaey. *Agrostis tenuis* grows similarly to some extent on the outskirts of the puffin ground, covering about 3%. Other species growing in the puffin ground, covering about 6% in all, are: *Rumex acetosa*, *Ranunculus acris* and *Cerastium caespitosum*. In the puffin ground it seems that *Cerastium* and *Poa trivialis* have given way to *Ranunculus* and *Rumex* since measured in 1933. Two years before our present observation, the grazing of sheep on the island ceased, and this has undoubtedly had some effect on the composition of vegetation. As there have been no sheep present for the last two years to hold the extensive growth of grass in check, the wilted grass accumulates to a still greater extent than before without any appreciable decomposition and forms a thick organic layer. Underneath this mat the sward may be stifled. Patches of decaying vegetation are thus to be seen in a number of places. To throw further light on the production of individual plant communities on Bjarnarey, the yield was measured. Samples taken from the puffin ground gave a yield of 4800 kg D.M. per hectare on the average. A sample taken from the dry meadowland gave substantially less, e.g. 2700 kg D.M. per hectare. Thus the yields are fully comparable with those obtained on cultivated land under regular application of fertilisers.

At Hvannhilla on the northern side of the island, the third association is to be found: the angelica clusters. This area is rather easily reached from the sea, but in general it is difficult to reach such associations which are situated on shelves and in niches on the cliff face. Hvannhilla slopes diagonally up the rock from the sea. At its lower extremity there is little vegetation; then comes a grass slope with a composition similar to that of the puffin ground. The angelica cluster is at the top of the incline, extending down along the cliff for a short distance. This covers an area of 420 sq. m. The dominant species *Angelica archangelica* was extremely luxuriant, about 120 cm high and with a coverage of 51%. Its associated species consisted of *Matricaria maritima* 12% and *Stellaria media* 14%, which form the undergrowth, and *Festuca rubra* 13%, which grows on the margins, while bare patches measured 10%. The soil of the angelica clusters was somewhat gravelly and fairly wet, for water drips constantly down the rock. Fulmar frequent this area in particular, supplying natural fertiliser. The angelica clusters consequently could be named the fulmar colony vegetation. Here some changes in distribution seem to have taken place since 1933. Three species—*Ranunculus acris*, *Sedum rosea* and *Cochlearia officinalis*—have disappeared, and other associated species become less frequent. Furthermore, the *Angelica* appears to have thinned somewhat during the 33 years between measurements.

ÁLSEY

Álsey is the third island in size, about 0.25 sq. km in area. It is very precipitous, surrounded by cliff on all sides except the northern. There is no level ground on the island apart from its extreme summit, where there is a patch of dry meadowland. This is very small in size. The dominating species of the dry meadowland are *Festuca rubra* 43%, *Poa pratensis* 37% and *Agrostis tenuis* 10%. On the crest of the island, however, *Poa pratensis* is dominant, and there is a similarity in vegetation there to the marginal strip mentioned in connection with the larger islands.

The puffin-ground vegetation is the dominating association of the island: *Festuca rubra* 80.5%, *Matricaria maritima* 3% and *Stellaria media* 6%. Bare patches measured 10.5% on the average and are most in evidence where the puffin nests are densest. There the associated species have the greatest ease in taking root. Altogether 25 species of vascular plants have been found on Álsey, including one not found elsewhere on the outer islands: *Saxifraga rivularis*. This grows in the so-called Vatnsgil, together with *Montia lamprosperma* and *Saxifraga caespitosa*. As the name indicates, there is a small trickle of water in this place.

SUDUREY

Sudurey is the fourth in order of size: about 0.20 sq. km in area. It is relatively high, 161 m, and surrounded by cliffs except on the southern side, where the only landing place is situated. This landing place faces the direction of the main breakers, making it extremely difficult to get ashore there. It rises in a steep slope that reaches to the summit of the island. At the bottom there is coastal cliff vegetation, reaching to a considerable height, about 50 m. Above this comes the puffin colony, which extends all the way to the top. On the northern side of the summit ridge, there is a steep bank of mixed dry meadowland with a gradient that becomes easier as it descends, giving way to the puffin ground. There is relatively little slope on the most northerly part of the island. Pure dry meadowland does not exist, only meadow-type margins to the puffin ground.

Point-measurements were taken on the steep slope below the summit. The dominant species of this marginal zone is *Festuca rubra* 58%, with the major associated species *Poa pratensis* 30% and *Agrostis tenuis* 10%. In the year 1965 point-measurement taken at the most northerly part of the island, close to the cliff edge, showed *Poa pratensis* to be dominant with 53%, while *Festuca rubra* was 43%. The marginal strip is very distinct there.

The principal association on the island is the puffin colony, where the dominant species is *Festuca rubra* 58% and associated species *Stellaria media* 32%, *Poa pratensis* 2.5% and *Matricaria maritima* 7.7%. In number of species Sudurey resembles Ellidaey, though not much more than half of its size. Altogether 23 species of vascular plants have been found there. Some moist spots occur on the island, namely on the sloping marginal zone to the north. In this area are present almost all the species of vascular plants to be found on the island, in addition to several species of moss.

BRANDUR

The island has an obvious crater formation and is only 0.1 sq. km in area. There is no level ground on it, only steep grass slopes and cliffs. The principal association is the puffin-ground vegetation. Its dominant species is *Festuca rubra* 60%; associated species are *Matricaria maritima* 23% and *Stellaria media* 9%. There is no appreciable dry meadowland on the island. *Poa pratensis* grows only on a patch of a few square metres on the crest of the island, where it covers about 27%. There is virtually no coastal cliff vegetation, but it is worth noting that there is a small skerry off the main island—actually a crater plug about 5 m high—where *Armeria maritima* grows in dense clusters, together with *Cochlearia officinalis* and *Puccinellia maritima*. *Armeria* is comparatively rare in the coastal cliff vegetation of the outer islands. Altogether 11 species of vascular plants have been observed on Brandur.

HELLISEY

This island is a small crater, about half of which has been eroded, so that the bowl is open on the south-western side facing the prevailing winds. Hellisey is only 0.1 sq. km in area, precipitous on the northern and western sides, but with a steep coastal slope, corresponding to the inner wall of the crater bowl, to the south. The principal association is the coastal cliff vegetation, found scattered along the cliffs with plants such as *Armeria maritima*, *Puccinellia maritima*, *Atriplex patula*, *Cochlearia officinalis* and *Plantago maritima*. High up on the island the puffin-ground vegetation is found. Its dominant species was *Festuca rubra*, about 45% average, with associated species *Matricaria maritima* 16%, *Atriplex patula* 3.5% and *Puccinellia maritima* 3%. Bare patches were extensive, or 33%. The puffin ground was completely honeycombed and much trodden by the birds. In many places the droppings had burned away all vegetation, especially where gannets, *Sula bassana*, had taken over parts of the puffin ground. It is worth noting that the *Puccinellia* and *Atriplex* grow well on the edges of areas of droppings and appear to tolerate the high fertility level of the gannet ground even better than the *Festuca*. No dry meadowland occurs on the island. Altogether nine species of vascular plants have been found there.

SÚLNASKER

Súlnasker is perpendicular on all sides, about 70 m high and 0.03 sq. km in area. On top of the skerry there is a ridge with some level ground on the summit and slopes to either side of it (Plate 12).

Dry meadowland does not occur. The puffin ground covers most of the skerry, but there is coastal cliff vegetation in a belt below the puffin ground. In several places there are large bare patches, where the gannets have colonised (Plate 13). The dominant species of the puffin-ground vegetation is *Festuca rubra*, with associated species *Stellaria media*, *Matricaria maritima* and *Cochlearia officinalis*. The *Festuca* is fairly dense on the level ground at the summit, but sparser on the slopes, where the associated species are more in evidence. It may be noted that to the south of the central ridge rain-water collects in a small depression, on the edges of which *Poa annua* was growing (Plate 14). In the outer margins of the puffin ground and towards the gannet ground *Puccinellia maritima*, *Atriplex patula* and *Cochlearia officinalis* were present. Altogether seven species of vascular plants have been found on Súlnasker.

GEIRFUGLASKER

Geirfuglasker is sheer on all sides, about 58 m high and 0.02 sq. km in area. The rock is for the most part level on top, with scattered vegetation which has clearly been considerably damaged by tephra from the Surtsey eruption.

Before this the *Puccinellia* seems to have formed continuous carpets of vegetation, but it was now smothered by the tephra. There was still some growth on higher points and at the cliff edge, where the tephra had not been able to lodge. Altogether four species of vascular plants were found: *Puccinellia maritima*, *Atriplex patula*, *Cochlearia officinalis* and *Matricaria maritima*. The last mentioned were in flower.

THRÍDRANGAR

This is a group of skerries to the north-west of the island of Heimaey. The highest of them, Vitadrangur, is about 40 m and rises sheer from the sea. Here two species of vascular plants have been found: *Puccinellia maritima* and *Cochlearia officinalis*, though less than a hundred individual plants of each species.

FAXASKER

Faxasker is to the north of Yztiklettur on Heimaey. It is rather low, not more than 10 m above sea-level and covered by the breakers in rough weather. There is a shelter for shipwrecked seamen on the rock, and also a light. Three species of vascular plants have been found there, though only a few individual plants of each: *Cochlearia officinalis*, *Puccinellia maritima* and *Stellaria media*.

NOTES ON THE FLORA OF THE SMALLER ISLANDS

On these Westman Islands the vegetation is prolific but scanty in species, with a total of only 33 species of vascular plants. On Ellidaey, the largest of the outer islands, the number of species is 23, but on the pinnacles of Geirfuglasker and Thrídrangar the species recorded were four and two respectively. The species found on each individual island are listed in Table 15.1.

An attempt was made to classify the species of the outer Westman Islands according to geographical distribution and life forms. The species are compared with those of four other Icelandic isolates. Three of these are tuff mountains isolated by alluvial gravel and sand, and situated on the mainland in the neighbourhood of Mýrdalur, southern Iceland. The number of species found were as follows: Pétursey 73, Hjörleifshöfdi 75, and Hafursey 89 species. The fourth isolate chosen for comparison is the island of Grímsey, situated off the north coast of Iceland with a total of 116 species (Table 15.2).

Table 15.1. *Floral list from eleven islets of the Westman Islands group*

Species	Life* forms	Surtsey	Ellidaey	Bjarnarey	Álsey	Sudurey	Brandur	Hellisey	Súlnasker	Geirfuglasker	Thrídrangar	Faxasker
Achillea millefolium	$H-E_3$			x	x	x						
Agrostis stolonifera	$H-E_3$			x	x	x						
Agrostis tenuis	$H-E_3$		x	x	x	x						
Angelica archangelica	$H-A_2$	x	x	x	x	x						
Anthoxanthum odoratum	$H-E_3$			x								
Armeria maritima	$CH-A_3$		x	x								
Atriplex patula	$TH-E_2$				x	x	x	x	x	x		
Cakile edentula	TH	x										
Carex maritima	$H-E_3$	x										
Cerastium caespitosum	$CH-E_3$		x	x	x	x	x					
Cochlearia officinalis	$H-E_4$	x	x	x	x	x	x	x	x	x	x	x
Cystopteris fragilis	$G-E_2$	x										
Elymus arenarius	$G-E_4$	x										
Equisetum arvense	$G-E_2$			x								
Euphrasia frigida	$TH-A_2$		x	x		x						
Festuca rubra	$H-E_4$	x	x	x	x	x	x	x	x			
Leodonton autumnalis	$H-E_3$		x	x	x	x						
Luzula multiflora	$H-E_3$			x								
Matricaria maritima	$H-E_3$	x	x	x	x	x	x	x	x	x		
Mertensia maritima	$H-E_3$	x										
Montia lamprosperma	$TH-E_4$			x	x	x						
Plantago maritima	$H-E_4$		x	x	x	x	x	x				
Poa annua	$TH-E_3$		x	x	x	x			x			
Poa pratensis	$G-E_3$		x	x	x	x	x	x				
Poa trivialis	$H-E_2$		x	x	x	x						
Potentilla anserina	$H-E_4$			x								
Puccinellia maritima	$H-E_3$	x	x	x	x	x	x	x	x	x	x	x
Ranunculus acris	$H-E_4$		x	x	x	x						
Ranunculus repens	$H-E_4$		x			x						
Rumex acetosa	$H-E_3$		x	x	x							
Sagina procumbens	$CH-E_3$		x	x	x	x						
Saxifraga caespitosa	$CH-A_3$		x	x	x							
Saxifraga rivularis	$H-A_3$					x						
Sedum roseum	$H-A_2$		x	x	x							
Silene maritima	$CH-A_1$		x	x	x	x	x					
Stellaria media	$TH-E_4$	x	x	x	x	x	x	x	x			x
Taraxacum acromauris	$H-E_2$		x	x	x	x						
Number of species per island		11	23	30	25	23	11	9	7	4	2	3
Area of islands in sq. km		2.50	0.46	0.32	0.25	0.20	0.10	0.13	0.04	0.02	0.01	0.01

* See Table 15.2 for definitions.

Table 15.2. *Life forms and number of vascular plant species from nine Westman Islands, three inland mountain isolates and Grímsey*

Locations	Number of species	A %	E %	PH %	CH %	H %	G %	TH %	HH %
Grímsey	116	42	58		15.5	61.2	12.0	7.7	5.2
Hafursey	89	39	61	1	27	58.4	6.7	8.0	5.2
Hjörleifshöfdi	75	36	64		26.6	54.6	9.3	9.3	
Pétursey	73	29	71		24.6	60.0	7	8	
Heimaey	150	26	74	0	13.4	61.7	8	13.4	3.4
Ellidaey	23	26	74		17	65	5	13	
Bjarnarey	30	20	80		17	63	7	13	
Álsey	25	20	80		12	68	4	16	
Sudurey	23	13	84		13	60	5	22	
Brandur	11	18	82		27	45	10	18	
Hellisey	9	10	90		11	55	11	22	
Súlnasker	7	0	100			57		43	
Geirfuglasker	4	0	100			75		25	
Thrídrangar	2	0	100			100			
Faxasker	3		100			70		30	
The small islands total	33	20	80		15	64	6	15	0

A	Arctic species	H	Hemicryptophytes
E	European species	G	Geophytes
PH	Pheophytes	TH	Therophytes
CH	Chamaephytes	HH	Hydrophytes, Helophytes

The comparison shows that the number of Arctic species increases with increased latitude, changing from no Arctic element in the flora of Súlnasker and Geirfuglasker to 42% Arctic species in the flora of Grímsey. The majority of the species of the outer Westman Islands, 74% to 100%, are of European type.

THE VEGETATION OF THE SMALLER ISLANDS

In general, the predominant vegetation on the larger islets are the grasses, especially *Festuca rubra*, which seems to be favoured by the environmental conditions present.

The surface of the islands is generally sloping towards the sea, preventing water from accumulating. During periods of drought, which can last for several weeks, the soil may become so dry that only the highly drought-resistant species survive.

In addition, the fertility level of the soil, the effect of the velocity and frequency of winds, the splashing of sea water, as well as the grazing of sheep, are important environmental factors and presumably account for the fact that no woody plants grow wild on the islands. The high precipitous cliffs, reaching considerable depths below sea-level and thus devoid of gravel beaches, exclude some coastal species and hinder dispersal by sea.

A review of the distribution of species in the principal association of the outer islands—the puffin ground and the dry meadowland—shows the dominant species of the former to be *Festuca rubra*, and of the latter, *Agrostis tenuis*. On the margins of the puffin ground *Poa pratensis* is dominant.

The difference in distribution of these species is hardly due to difference in temperature, humidity and light, as these seem to be more or less the same in both types of associations. More likely it is due to a difference in fertility level of the soil. No qualitative analysis of the soil was made, but from simple observation it is clear that the quantity of droppings in the two principal associations differs considerably. In the puffin ground itself, which the birds constantly frequent, the amount of droppings must be many times greater than that in the dry meadowland. In fact, where the puffin nests are densest, the growth has been destroyed by droppings. Judging by this, the *Festuca* and its associated species are most manure tolerant. After these comes the *Poa*, which flourishes in the marginal zones, but the *Agrostis* is dominant in the dry meadowland where droppings are scantiest. This is especially evident on the largest of the islands, Ellidaey, where the dry meadowland is the most extensive. As the islands decrease in area, the amount of dry meadowland gets less and the proportion of puffin-ground vegetation to the whole increases, until it becomes the predominant association. On islands of medium size, such as Álsey and Sudurey, true dry meadowland disappears and a marginal strip takes its place. Three factors are paramount in determining the extent of the puffin ground. Firstly, there must be sufficient depth of soil for the birds to dig their burrows, up to one metre. Secondly, there must be a view to the sea. Thirdly, there must be an adequate slope, for the puffin must be able to jump downwards in order to take flight. From this, it will be seen that the puffin-ground vegetation is to be found especially on the seaward slopes, while the dry meadowland occurs in the middle of the island where there is level ground, or in hollows and places where the soil is shallow. As the islands become yet smaller, the extent of the puffin ground is reduced and coastal cliff vegetation takes over. This is owing to the increased effect of wind and sea, which makes the formation of top-soil more difficult. It is also clear that the number of species increases roughly in proportion to the area of the islands and the corresponding variety of growth conditions. It must be mentioned, however, that the number of species and composition of associations are also affected by microclimatic factors, such as humidity, shelter and exposure. The angelica clusters constitute a localised association to the northern side of the islands, where the sun is least effective and there is sufficient moisture. The dominant species of this association is

Plate 12. Súlnasker

*Plate 13. Young gan-
nets, Sula bassana, on
Súlnasker*

Plate 14. The wet spot on Súlnasker with low spear grass, Poa annua. *The puffin-ground vegetation in the background*

Angelica archangelica, a species that flourishes in low temperatures but requires a fairly large amount of moisture and a soil with a rather high fertility content. Sheep are very partial to the *Angelica* and keep it down wherever they can get to it. For this reason it is only found on cliff faces and clefts in the rock where it is hard to reach.

It can be regarded as certain that the grazing of sheep has had a material effect on the vegetation of the islands, both through their introduction of seeds and also by selective grazing, for example of the *Angelica*. With the single exception of Ellidaey, the islands are now no longer used for grazing, and this is bound to bring some changes in the vegetation. The areas of vegetation on these islands will thus tend to revert to their natural balance. Sheep, when grazing, consume part of the annual growth which would otherwise wilt. A great mass of wilted grass suffocates the living, resulting in bare patches as observed in Bjarnarey.

Differences between the islands in number of species and associations have been discussed above with reference to varying conditions of growth. It must, however, be borne in mind that the dispersal routes to individual islands vary in distance, and also that the period of time elapsed since the formation of individual islands in the group may vary considerably. Thus, Ellidaey is relatively poor in species in view of its size and proximity to the mainland, which might seem to indicate that it was of comparatively more recent formation. Its dry meadowland being composed of only a few species might indicate that it has not reached the same advancement in succession as that of Bjarnarey. The more complex dry meadowland association on Bjarnarey may thus be a more advanced succession, or it may be a result of special micro-climatic factors such as the effect of shelter, conditions of growth not existing elsewhere among the outer islands.

It is evident that all these special environmental factors cause great limitations to the number of species and their associations in the islands.

Although the migration of plants is restricted to some extent by the isolation of the islands, the flora of each individual island has to be regarded as being primarily governed by the present environmental conditions. Most of the old volcanic islands are of a comparatively stable topography with a vegetation that has become stabilised in four major types of climax communities in their respective habitats. These have to some extent formed a zonation extending from the splash zone at the lower level with transition through the fertile soil of the puffin ground to the dry lands of the upper parts of the islands. In contrast to these stable communities, the newly formed island of Surtsey, which was completely bare, has at present only a few pioneer plants. Through a study of the colonisation of the biota of Surtsey a great deal may be learned about the ecology and the process of succession on the older islands.

REFERENCES

JOHNSEN, B., 'Observation on the vegetation of the Westman Islands', *Societas Scientiarum Islandica, Rit,* **22** (1937)

FRIDRIKSSON, S. and JOHNSEN, B., 'Preliminary report on the vascular flora of the lesser Westman Islands', *Surtsey Res. Progr. Rep.,* **2**, 45–58 (1966)

FRIDRIKSSON, S. and JOHNSEN, B., 'On the vegetation of the outer Westman Islands', *Surtsey Res. Progr. Rep.,* **3**, 20–36 (1967)

FRIDRIKSSON, S. and JOHNSEN, B., 'The vascular flora of the outer Westman Islands', *Societas Scientiarum Islandica, Greinar,* **4**, No. 3, 37–67 (1967)

16

THE VEGETATION OF HEIMAEY

The study of the vegetation of Heimaey was begun in the summer of 1969. The vegetation had previously been investigated in 1933. However, during the time that had since elapsed some changes might have occurred, and it was interesting to compare this advanced vegetation with the primitive state of communities on Surtsey. It was also valuable to know the exact number of species growing on Heimaey with regard to dispersal of plants to Surtsey. Thus, it was decided to try to make a thorough botanical survey and a fairly accurate vegetation map of the island. During the summer of 1969 preliminary measurements were made of all the plant-communities, but the weather then was extraordinarily unfavourable, so that less was accomplished than intended. In the summer of 1970 investigation and sketching of the communities, from which the map was later prepared, were completed. That summer most of the island was investigated. Aerial photographs of the area were used in the field and compared with the landscape on the site while the vegetation was measured. The distribution of every community was then marked on the photos.

The sociological measurements were in both years performed in accordance with the methods of Hult–Sernander Du Rietz. After the measurements had been carried out, the communities were grouped and identification letters allocated for relevant communities. It should be mentioned that a closer study proved it was very difficult to classify some of the areas into communities, as they were not clearly defined. The boundaries between the communities are therefore in some cases rather arbitrary.

THE TOPOGRAPHY

As already stated, the island has been formed by volcanic eruptions at the end of the last ice age, and subsequently. The volcano Helgafell (Holy Mountain) is situated to the south-east. The island is fringed on most sides with steep cliffs, but there is a sand beach on the isthmus between the cliffs Heimaklettur and Háin and between Stórhöfdi and the main part of the island, known as Klaufin. In some places the cliffs rise high and form shapely and striking mountains. South of Helgafell the ground is flat, and a large part of the island was covered with old lava on which there is a good deal of vegetation. Some shelter is found in two grassy dells, but otherwise the ground is rather barren.

The landscape has in many places been affected by man and animals. For instance, roads have been laid across the island, and road-building material has been taken from the eastern slopes of Helgafell. The town is situated on the north slope of Helgafell and an airfield has been built on the island.

THE VEGETATION

The vegetation may be divided into eight communities: the dry meadow-land; the herb slope; the puffin ground; the gravelly flat; the heath; the sand beach; the bog, and the cliff community. The dry meadowland covers the largest area of land and is dominated by grasses.

The herb slope has the greatest variety of species. The puffin ground shows very little variety of species but excellent growth. This community is usually found on slopes. Gravelly flat communities are rather widespread, and until recently there has been considerable erosion in this area, probably because of the encroachment of sheep. There are many species, but typical gravel plants are the most common. The heath community is mostly found in the dry lava fields.

There is little coastal vegetation as such, for the island is largely fringed with steep cliffs, so that the coastal vegetation merges with cliff vegetation. There is, however, a sand beach with *Honckenya peploides*, *Mertensia maritima* and *Elymus arenarius* on Thraelaeidi and Klaufin.

Table 16.1. List of vascular plants from Heimaey

Achillea millefolium
Agrostis canina
Agrostis stolonifera
Agrostis tenuis
Alchemilla alpina
Alchemilla sp.
Alopecurus aequalis
Alopecurus geniculatis
Angelica archangelica
Anthoxanthum odoratum
Armeria maritima
Atriplex glabriuscula
Avenochloa pubescens
Bartsia alpina
Botrychium lunaria
Bromus inermis
Cakile edentula
Calluna vulgaris
Capsella bursa-pastoris
Cardamine hirsuta
Cardamine pratensis
Cardaminopsis petrea
Carex capillaris
Carex flacca
Carex lyngbyei
Carex maritima
Carex nigra
Carex rariflora
Cerastium alpinum
Cerastium cerastoides
Cerastium fontanum
Chenopodium album
Cirsium arvense
Coeloglossum viride
Cystopteris fragilis
Dactylis glomerata
Draba incana
Deschampsia caespitosa
Eleocharis uniglumis
Elymus arenarius
Empetrum hermaphroditum
Epilobium collinum
Equisetum arvense

Equisetum palustre
Equisetum pratense
Erigeron boreale
Eriophorum angustifolium
Eriophorum scheuchzeri
Euphrasia frigida
Festuca rubra
Festuca vivipara
Filipendula ulmaria
Galium normanii
Galium verum
Gentianella amarella
Gentianella aurea
Gentianella campestris
Gnaphalium uliginosum
Hieracium sp.
Honckenya peploides
Juncus articulatus
Juncus bufonius
Juncus trifidus
Kobresia myosuroides
Koenigia islandica
Lathyrus maritimus
Lathyrus pratensis
Leontodon autumnalis
Linum catharticum
Lolium perenne
Luzula multiflora
Luzula spicata
Matricaria maritima★
Matricaria matricarioides
Mertensia maritima
Myosotis arvensis
Oxyria digyna
Parnassia palustris
Phleum pratense
Pinguicula vulgaris
Plantago lanceolata
Plantago maritima
Poa annua
Poa glauca
Poa pratensis
Poa trivialis

Polygonum aviculare
Polygonum viviparum
Polypodium vulgare
Potentilla anserina
Potentilla crantzii
Prunella vulgaris
Puccinellia maritima
Puccinellia retroflexa
Ranunculus acris
Ranunculus repens
Rhinanthus minor
Rubus saxatilis
Rumex acetosa
Rumex acetosella
Rumex longifolius
Sagina nodosa
Sagina procumbens
Salix herbacea
Saxifraga caespitosa
Saxifraga hypnoides
Saxifraga nivalis
Sedum acre
Sedum rosea
Sedum villosum
Selaginella selaginoides
Senecio vulgaris
Sieglingia decumbens
Silene acaulis
Silene maritima
Spergula arvensis
Stellaria media
Succisa pratensis
Taraxacum sp.
Thalictrum alpinum
Thymus drucei
Trifolium repens
Triglochin palustre
Trisetum spicatum
Urtica urens
Veronica officinalis
Vicia cracca
Vicia sepium
Viola canina

★ syn. Tripleurospermum maritimum.

There are two boggy patches in Herjólfsdalur valley where some species, not found elsewhere on the island, are growing, but this community seems to be deteriorating.

The cliff vegetation is common, especially in and near the breeding areas of the fulmar and kittiwake.

The vascular species of Heimaey are listed in Table 16.1. The species which were found growing in the various societies are dealt with on the following pages. The distribution of the societies and the area of the various communities can be seen on the accompanying map (Figure 16.1).

THE DRY MEADOWLAND COMMUNITY

The community of the dry meadowland, being the most widespread, may be subdivided into four societies according to the predominant types and the composition of the species. A1 *Agrostis tenuis—Anthoxanthum odoratum* society and A4 *Festuca vivipara—Anthoxanthum odoratum* society are fairly similar, but the former is more developed and on moister soil. A2 is a *Festuca rubra* society and A3 is a *Festuca rubra–Poa pratensis* society. These are both found on rather similar soils.

THE HERB SLOPE

The herb slope is sometimes regarded as a type of meadowland community, but should possibly be considered a separate community.

A characteristic of this society is the great variety of species, and especially the herbs which are more numerous and widespread than in other societies. Some of the most conspicuous are: *Achillea millefolium, Plantago lanceolata, Rhinanthus minor* and *Taraxacum* sp.

This society is found on dry, sandy slopes, often facing south. In such habitats the passage of sheep and people frequently disturbs the vegetation.

THE PUFFIN-GROUND COMMUNITY

It is doubtful whether this kind of vegetation should be regarded as a separate community, but although perhaps artificial this convenient classification is used. It is noteworthy that where the puffin starts to nest the slopes retain to some extent their vegetation characteristics, i.e. the large amount of manure makes the number of species fewer than otherwise, and associated species are more widespread than they are outside such habitats, e.g. *Stellaria media,*

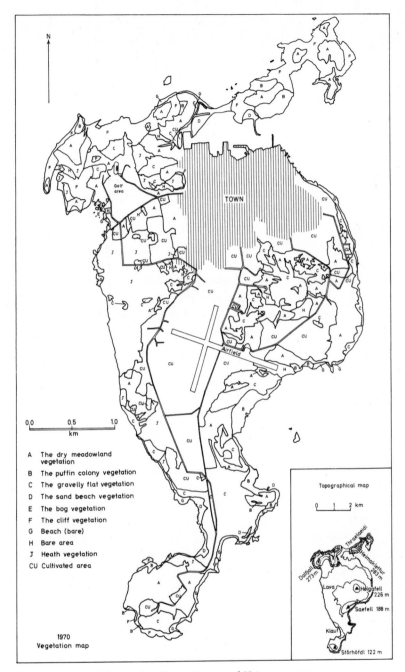

Figure 16.1. *Vegetation map of Heimaey, 1970*

Legend (within the map):

A The dry meadowland vegetation
B The puffin colony vegetation
C The gravelly flat vegetation
D The sand beach vegetation
E The bog vegetation
F The cliff vegetation
G Beach (bare)
H Bare area
J Heath vegetation
CU Cultivated area

1970
Vegetation map

Topographical map

157

Rumex acetosa. The most abundant species of the puffin ground are: *Festuca rubra, Poa pratensis* and *Poa trivialis.*

THE GRAVELLY FLAT COMMUNITY

The gravelly flats are rather variable and the number of species does not give a true cross section. It is most abundant near the edges of a denser vegetation. Species are: *Cardaminopsis petrea, Cerastium* sp. and *Thymus drucei.*

A characteristic feature is the open soil with the low frequency and cover of plants. Some species have a clustered distribution, i.e. *Armeria maritima, Silene acaulis* and *Silene maritima.* Others have a more regular or random distribution. There is an obvious resemblance between the gravelly flat community and the cliff community, especially where there are bigger boulders among the gravel. The gravelly flats are open areas, which have lost the fertile top layer of soil through erosion. In areas where the erosion is recent, the gravel is mixed with the remnants of the topsoil. In this 'flag' type of soil *Cerastium caespitosum* and *Sedum villosum* are found growing.

THE HEATH VEGETATION

Where the soil is very dry, the heath vegetation gradually takes over the dry meadowland. The heath vegetation can either be found on sloped or flat land. Mostly it is found in the old lava covering the mid-west part of the island, and also on the top of the mountains.

The characteristics of the heath vegetation are mainly: high coverage of *Empetrum hermaphroditum* and/or *Salix herbacea.* The division between societies is partly based on the presence of either of these species. Also characteristic is high coverage of mosses (*Racomitrium* sp. in the lava) and the existence of *Kobresia myosuroides* and *Luzula multiflora* and *L. spicata.*

Empetrum hermaphroditum society and *Salix herbacea* society are in many ways similar, of like composition and, in fact, often merge into one another. *Salix herbacea,* however, is more to be found on flat land and its productivity is greater than in the *Empetrum* society, where the vegetation is frequently less dense.

THE SAND BEACH COMMUNITY

It is difficult to use any regular measurements for the vegetation in these areas, because of the very uneven distribution of the plants. Near the sea, about 5 m from high-tide mark, may be seen the first wisps of *Honckenya peploides* and *Mertensia maritima*. *Honckenya* forms larger wisps than *Mertensia*, and in some places quite shapely hummocks. A little higher up, and among the hummocks, grows *Cakile edentula*. Still higher up are dunes, in which the *Elymus arenarius* predominates.

Sand beach is found chiefly in two places, i.e. at Thraelaeidi *en route* to Heimaklettur, and at Klaufin beside the isthmus on Stórhöfdi.

THE BOG COMMUNITY

Hardly any bogs are to be found in the Westman Islands. There are two small patches in Herjólfsdalur near the sea, where traces of bog can be discerned. It would seem that water collects here. It is difficult to estimate the size of this bog because it gradually merges with the surrounding vegetation. The uppermost patch was more typical and larger, and the water level higher. The patches were quite separated from each other by a strip of grass.

THE CLIFF COMMUNITY

Cliffs encircle most of the island. In all these cliffs, and in many other places, birds breed in great numbers, especially the fulmar and the kittiwake. In the nesting grounds and around them, a large amount of bird droppings clearly has a great influence on the composition of the vegetation. Beneath those areas in the cliffs where there is an inward slope or there are for other reasons no bird droppings, there is here and there a rather broad belt, about 1 m, of *Atriplex glabruiscula*.

On the ledges and under the cliffs there is, as stated above, a large amount of bird droppings. In many of these habitats are found *Angelica archangelica*, together with *Ranunculus acris*, *Rumex acetosa* and *Matricaria maritima*. This may be considered a separate community, which has previously been named the angelica cluster. On the edges and in the clefts of the cliffs *Sedum rosea* is often found to be the dominant species.

The vegetation on Heimaey shows much sign of trampling and encroachment by animals, so that a natural composition of vegetation is hardly to be found except on the cliffs.

Many species, which have been found either on cultivated land or in the town of Heimaey, or where the ground cover has been disturbed by man, are not necessarily mentioned in the description of the societies. These were, however, recorded and are listed in Table 16.1.

In the town there are, for instance, patches of *Matricaria matricarioides*, *Poa annua*, *Lolium perenne* and other species. Above the Fridarhöfn, Peace Harbour, was a large area mostly covered with *Urtica urens* and *Euphrasia frigida*. Various other plants were found in the vicinity of the harbour. Plants cultivated in gardens or which grew in rubbish dumps are not included in the lists of plants.

THE ERUPTION ON HEIMAEY

Ever since the eruption on Surtsey started in 1963, the scientists studying the volcanic outbreak, the formation of the island and the colonisation of life on Surtsey had used Heimaey as a place of embarkation for their transport to the new volcanic island. Various vehicles were used for this final step in the numerous expeditions, such as helicopters and small single-engined aeroplanes, coastguard vessels and pilot boats, but mostly small fishing-boats and rubber dinghies (Figure 4.4a).

Landing on Surtsey was often difficult. The sandy beach serving as a runway was strewn with rocks, which the air-pilot had to avoid, and during rough seas the approach to the shore by boat was often dangerous as the waves swept along the coast, often capsizing the rubber rafts used as ferries. But the distance from Heimaey is only 20 km, and the town there had both an airfield and an excellent harbour, so that trips between the islands were frequent during the summer when fresh water and food supplies had to be shipped to Surtsey, or when samples needed to be taken for closer investigation to the small laboratory of the town's natural history museum and aquarium.

Heimaey, being the largest island of the group with rich vegetation and animal life, was also obviously the place from whence life would most likely spread to Surtsey. Mindful of this, the flora and the fauna of Heimaey were also investigated and the island's vegetation mapped, as was described in a previous chapter. As Heimaey had a town with over 5000 inhabitants and a busy harbour, it was also expected that some of the human activities there might influence life on Surtsey. This, however, has been negligible except for some garbage cast overboard from boats or into the harbour that may eventually be washed by currents to the Surtsey shores.

During our investigations in the area, no one could have expected any influence of volcanic activity on life from the secure island of Heimaey and its Peace Harbour. Admittedly, Mount Helgafell bore witness to the volcanic origin of the island, but it had been quiet for over 5000 years.

It was therefore a great surprise and a shock to everyone when shortly after midnight on 23 January 1973 a volcanic outbreak started at the edge of the town. Most of the inhabitants were sound asleep, and only a few witnessed the first phase of the eruption when the level meadow south-east of the town started swelling up.

The sward of a farmer's hayfield was torn asunder and the particles thrown into the air. Then suddenly the surface was ripped open like flesh cut by the stroke of a blade and the lava oozed out as blood from a wound. The fissure that had cracked open was almost 2 km long, running from north-north-east to south-south-west, east of Helgafell, and from it gushed flaming gases and glowing cinder through numerous craters (Plate 15). The town was evacuated during the first night and the people were brought to the mainland by numerous fishing boats and aircraft. But a rescue crew of a few hundred men stayed on the island to try to salvage valuable belongings from the houses.

Lava began to flow out of the fissure towards the sea on the north-eastern side of the island, gradually forming a lava tongue of over 2 sq. km in area. In early February a lava stream flowing to the north threatened to block the entrance to the harbour, which would have been disastrous for the community, as the fishing industry and the prosperity of the islanders is based on the sheltered harbour. The lava advanced far into the sea, crushing the telephone and electricity cables and the mains which carried running water to Heimaey from the mainland.

In the beginning there was a constant shower of pumice from the fissure which piled up all around. Then, gradually, the activities concentrated in one of the central craters and a 200 m high mountain cone piled up (Plate 16). This crater, which was later named Eldfell, spouted a constant shower of pumice over the town and after a while buried the streets and houses (Plate 17). By the end of January more than 120 houses were lost. Most of them had been buried under pumice or covered by lava. Others had burned when hit by the 1000 °C hot embers and spatters of molten lava, which fell in showers on the roofs or through the windows. Some houses cracked and caved in from the weight of pumice collecting on their roofs.

In the middle of February volcanic gases with carbon dioxide, carbon monoxide and sulphuric compounds started streaming out from under the lava. The gas was heavy and crept along the ground, filling depressions and cellars. It soon became quite dangerous for all living beings attempting to enter houses in some of the town's low-lying streets.

The pumice burying houses located in the easternmost part of town was over 40 m thick, while an advancing lava front constantly threatened the town itself, pushing its centre forward towards the harbour and the precious freezing-plants.

The rescue crews fought a courageous battle to halt this advance by bull-dozing up ramparts and barriers of pumice and pumping sea-water on to

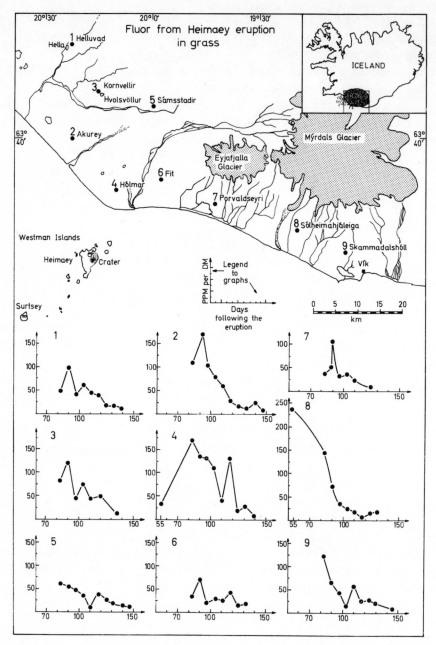

Figure 16.2. Map of the sites for the collection of grass and graphs of the measurement of its contamination by fluoride brought in by ash from the Heimaey eruption in 1973

the hot lava in order to cool the molten current. This way it was possible to change the course of the lava. Finally, in the early summer the volcanic activity ceased and part of the town had been saved.

Before the eruption there had been some farming on Heimaey, but when pumice started covering fields and pastures and when the islanders had to evacuate, it was foreseen that it would be difficult to keep animals on the island in the near future. Therefore sheep and ponies were transported to the mainland, as well as the pets.

Although the main pumice pile lay over the town and the eastern part of the island, it had also spread in varying quantities onto other areas of Heimaey. Some ash had fallen on the rocks on nearby islands and some was carried with the wind to the mainland. The fine ash particles contained fluoride that contaminated water and vegetation, which became unhealthy for consumption, and in the spring the farm animals of the southernmost lowland areas of the mainland, facing Heimaey, had to be kept indoors and fed on the last year's hay crop (Figure 16.2).

The eruption on Heimaey was indeed catastrophic both for the islanders, who lost their homes and livelihood, as well as for the Icelandic nation as a whole, having the main centre of its fishing industry paralysed.

Over 300 houses had been burned or buried under ash and many more were damaged. A section of the town had become another Pompeii (Plate 18).

In the summer of 1973 the restoration of the town began and some of the islanders returned. The pumice was cleaned from the streets and from some of the houses. The story goes that a puffin also returned to seek its old breeding hole. And as it was full of pumice the bird started digging until its feet were bleeding. In the spring plants began their growth and reached for light. Some were too deeply buried in the pumice. Others managed to break the surface to enjoy the long daylight. The effect on wild life had mostly been local on the eastern part of Heimaey. Other regions were less affected and on the outer islands life proceeded in a normal way.

REFERENCES

JOHNSEN, A., *Eldar í Heimaey*. Almenna Bókafélagid, Reykjavik, 190 (1973)
JOHNSEN, B., 'Observations on the vegetation of the Westman Islands', *Societas Scientiarum Islandica, Rit*, **22** (1937)
EYJÓLFSSON, G. Á., *Vestmannaeyjar*, Ísafold, Reykjavik, 368 (1973)
FRIDRIKSSON, S., BJARNASON, Á. H. and SVEINBJÖRNSSON, B., 'On the vegetation of Heimaey, preliminary report', *Surtsey Res. Progr. Rep.*, **6**, 34–36 (1972)
FRIDRIKSSON, S., SVEINBJÖRNSSON, B. and MAGNÚSSON, S., 'On the vegetation of Heimaey II', *Surtsey Res. Progr. Rep.*, **6**, 36–54 (1972)
GUNNARSSON, A., 'Volcano. Ordeal by fire in Iceland's Westman Islands', *Iceland Review*, Reykjavik, 96 (1973)

163

17

THE SOUTHERN COAST OF ICELAND

The insular eruptions had a negligible effect on the southern coast of the Icelandic mainland. Ash and fumes damaged vegetation and roofs of houses to some degree, while pumice floated along the shore and became deposited on the beach and in inlets along the adjacent shores.

This coast had often been affected to a greater extent by volcanic outbreaks. Even in historic times craters had erupted from under the glacial dome of Eyjafjalla and Mýrdalsjökull, and great floods had rushed to the shore sweeping away all life on the plains and carrying ash and pumice towards the ocean. The present beach is formed from this black tephra. In other places there are alluvial deposits from the glacial rivers forming low sandy beaches, or there are lava flows with steep edges and tuff mountain stacks with cliffs descending right down into the sea.

On the southern coast of Iceland ecological studies were undertaken during the summer months of July and August 1968, for the purpose of making a provisional survey of vegetation with regard to dispersal of plants and plant colonisation on the island of Surtsey.

Observations were made at 34 places along the south coast, from the fishing village of Thorlákshöfn in the west and as far east as the village of Vík in Mýrdal. Efforts were made to select the observation points at fairly regular intervals, although account had to be taken of where access to the coast was convenient.

The method of research was such that the topography and the substrate of the coast were primarily investigated and described. Further study depended on the type of coast. Where mountains or cliffs descended straight into the sea, it was considered sufficient to list the species growing nearest to the sea. Where there was a sandy beach or low lava protruding into the sea, observations commenced nearest the sea and then proceeded inland. Species were enumerated on a transect diagonally from the shore, and attempts were made where possible to obtain a survey of zonation of the vegetation. The transects varied on length, depending on the width of the coastal region. Studies were confined to the coastal area, which was often bordered by grass or moorland vegetation. The method used in measuring vegetation cover

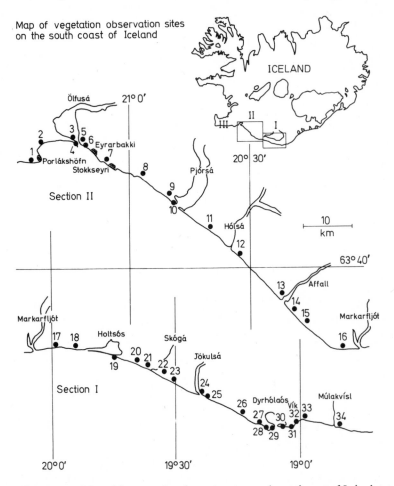

Figure 17.1. Map of the vegetation observation sites on the south coast of Iceland

Table 17.1. List of vascular plants found on the south coast of Iceland

Species / Site No.	1	2	3	4	5	6	7	8	9	10	11	12	13	14	15	16	17	18	19	20	21	22	23	24	25	26	27	28	29	30	31	32	33	34
Achillea millefolium																					x													
Agropyron repens						x	x																											
Agrostis stolonifera	x							x		x	x		x					x	x				x	x	x	x					x	x		x
Agrostis tenuis	x						x	x		x	x	x	x					x	x	x				x						x	x	x	x	x
Alopecurus geniculatus							x													x														
Angelica archangelica			x																					x			x			x	x	x		
Anthoxanthum odoratum																								x						x				
Arabis alpina																																		
Arenaria norvegica	x																																	
Armeria maritima	x	x	x					x		x			x								x	x	x	x	x	x				x	x	x		x
Atriplex patula		x					x																											
Botrychium lunaria																													x					
Calamagrostis neglecta		x		x	x	x	x	x				x	x																					
Cakile edentula																		x									x							
Capsella bursa-pastoris							x	x																										
Cardaminopsis petraea	x	x	x									x	x									x	x	x	x	x					x	x		x
Carex lyngbyei											x											x												
Carex maritima													x							x		x		x									x	x
Carex nigra											x	x																						
Cerastium caespitosum ssp. scandicum	x						x																	x						x				
Cochlearia officinalis								x																										
Cystopteris fragilis ssp. eufragilis																																		
Deschampsia caespitosa																											x				x	x		x
Draba incana												x																		x	x			
Eleocharis uniglumis												x																						
Elymus arenarius	x	x	x	x	x	x	x	x	x	x	x	x	x	x	x	x	x	x	x	x	x	x	x	x	x	x								
Epilobium collinum																												x						
Equisetum arvense											x	x							x	x	x					x						x		
Equisetum palustre											x	x								x														x

166

Plate 15. The fissure formed during the eruption on Heimaey, 23 January 1973 (Photo: S. Einarsson)

Plate 16. The new mountain Eldfell has been built up and a part of the town is under lava. Helgafell in the foreground (Photo: S. Einarsson)

Plate 17. Houses in the town of Heimaey threatened by glowing magma splashes (Photo: S. Einarsson)

Plate 18. An aerial view of Heimaey during summer 1973 after the eruption

Table 17.1 (continued)

Species	1	2	3	4	5	6	7	8	9	10	11	12	13	14	15	16	17	18	19	20	21	22	23	24	25	26	27	28	29	30	31	32	33	34
Euphrasia frigida																																x	x	
Festuca rubra v. *mutica*	x	x	x		x	x	x	x		x	x	x	x	x								x	x	x	x		x				x	x		x
Festuca vivipara																								x										
Galium boreale												x																						
Galium verum ssp. *euverum*	x			x		x		x		x		x											x			x					x	x		
Hieracium sp.		x																											x		x	x	x	
Honckenya peploides	x	x	x	x	x	x	x	x	x	x	x	x	x	x		x	x	x			x	x	x	x	x				x		x			x
Juncus alpinus ssp. *nodulosus*																				x														
Juncus arcticus								x				x							x															
Juncus ranarius																																		
Lathyrus maritimus v. *glaber*				x		x																												
Leontodon autumnalis			x			x	x																								x	x		
Ligusticum scoticum																															x			
Luzula multiflora																															x			
Luzula spicata	x																														x			
Matricaria maritima			x																							x					x			
Matricaria matricarioides	x																															x	x	
Mertensia maritima	x						x		x									x	x							x		x			x	x		x
Myosotis arvensis																															x	x		x
Oxyria digyna																																		
Parnassia palustris												x																						
Plantago major ssp. *eumajor*																															x			
Plantago maritima	x				x		x	x					x								x	x	x	x	x	x					x	x		x
Plantago lanceolata																															x	x		x
Poa alpina																																		x
Poa annua																			x	x														
Poa glauca	x																							x								x	x	
Poa pratensis ssp. *irrigata*		x				x																				x		x			x	x		x
Poa pratensis ssp. *eupratensis*																										x		x			x	x		x
Polygonum aviculare		x	x				x																											

167

Table 17.1 (continued)

Species	1	2	3	4	5	6	7	8	9	10	11	12	13	14	15	16	17	18	19	20	21	22	23	24	25	26	27	28	29	30	31	32	33	34
Polygonum viviparum																																		x
Potentilla anserina ssp. euanserina		x	x		x	x	x	x		x		x								x	x			x		x		x		x	x	x		
Puccinellia maritima							x	x										x	x											x		x		
Puccinellia retroflexa	x																													x				
Ranunculus acris ssp.· boreanus							x																	x						x		x		
Ranunculus acris v. pumillus												x										x	x							x		x		
Rumex acetosa																						x	x	x		x		x		x	x	x		
Rumex acetosella (incl. R. tenuifolius)	x	x	x			x						x	x							x	x	x	x	x		x							x	x
Rumex longifolius																				x						x		x		x	x	x		
Sagina procumbens			x																	x						x		x		x	x	x		x
Saxifraga nivalis																																x	x	
Saxifraga rivularis																																		
Sedum acre																								x								x	x	
Sedum rosea																											x			x	x	x		
Sedum villosum																																		
Senecio vulgaris																										x		x				x		x
Silene acaulis	x																																	
Silene maritima	x	x	x		x	x	x			x		x	x	x						x	x	x	x	x		x				x	x	x	x	x
Stellaria media																										x		x		x	x	x		
Taraxacum sp.			x									x												x	x	x		x		x				
Thymus drucei	x										x	x												x	x	x		x		x				
Urtica urens								x																										
Total of 82 species **TOTAL**	19	10	10	19	5	13	9	23	14	3	11	20	14	2	1	2	2	9	16	11	10	14	19	12	0	2	36	32	12	21				

168

was such that the cover within a quadrat of 1 sq. m was estimated. Five such adjacent quadrats were investigated at each observation site, and an average found for these five quadrats of each site. The vegetation cover was estimated in units of not lesss than 5%. The observation sites are marked on the accompanying map (Figure 17.1), and the species discovered are listed in Table 17.1.

The types of coast at the 34 observation sites may be divided into four main categories:

I. Sandy shore: This type was recorded at 27 observation sites; (2, 3, (4), (5), 6, (7), 9, (10), 11, 12, 13, 14, 15, 16, 17, 18, 19, 20, 21, 22, 23, 25, 26, 27, 30, 33, and 34 on Figure 17.1). The numbers in brackets indicate sites which fall into two categories.

This type of coast is the most characteristic for the south shore of Iceland. These shores are often such that *Cakile edentula*, *Mertensia* and *Honckenya peploides*—either one, two or all three species—are found in a zone nearest the sea. The next zone inland is then usually dominated by *Elymus arenarius*, frequently mixed with the above-mentioned three species and perhaps other species as distance from the sea increases.

II. River mouths were studied at four sites ((4), (5), (10), and 24). All the estuaries studied are bordered with sandbanks, sometimes with irregular gravel. The vegetation is extremely scanty on the sandspits as well as on the riverbanks, and a zonation is often obscure, where *Elymus arenarius* is commonly mixed with *Mertensia* and *Honckenya*, *Cakile* and a few grass species.

III. Lava protruding into the sea was found at two sites ((7) and 8), where it forms numerous skerries. The innermost skerries are often rich in vegetation. The dominant species is *Puccinellia maritima*, often associated with *Polygonum aviculare* and *Plantago maritima*. Behind the skerries is a sandy shore scattered with seaweed and with a dense vegetation of different coastal species mixed with various others.

IV. Mountains or sheer cliffs were observed at four sites (28, 29, 31, and 32). The mountains, which are of tuff, are sheer or scree-covered, mostly without vegetation in the splashing zone. Above this zone various grass species are found growing, associated with such species as *Angelica archangelica* and *Sedum rosea*.

Finally, there is an intermediary stage between III and IV at site 1, where there are sand dunes on a lava base which forms cliffs at the seashore or is broken up into boulders. These are devoid of vegetation, but farther inland various coastal species are growing in mixed communities.

REFERENCES

FRIDRIKSSON, S., RICHTER, S. H. and BJARNASON, A. H., 'Preliminary studies of the vegetation of the southern coast of Iceland', *Surtsey Res. Progr. Rep.*, **5**, 20–29 (1970)

18

SOME
CONCLUSIONS
AND
SPECULATIONS

THE DISPERSAL

In these last chapters I have mostly dealt with the study of higher plants on the adjacent islands and the southern shore of the mainland, but an investigation of the mosses and lichens has also been carried out, although these studies are not as far advanced as those of vascular plants. A thorough study of the marine algae on the various islands and the southern shore of Iceland has also been performed. Similarly the marine fauna in the archipelago is getting fairly well known through various biological research work. In addition to this the entomologists have investigated the terrestrial invertebrates of the different islands as well as on the southern mainland. Furthermore, the bird life of these areas has been under a continuous scrutiny. Besides this the geological examinations of the Westman Islands have also received great attention by the geologists who continue their research of the area. Thus the volcanic origin and development of the islands are by now rather well understood.

Oceanographic phenomena are under routine observation, and similarly there are permanent meteorological recordings carried out in the area. Thus the Westman Islands have awakened the interest of scholars of various disciplines who have accumulated great knowledge about life and its environment in the archipelago.

As the general direction of ocean currents around the islands is fairly well known one could predict the course of drifting objects in the area. The westward trend of the current, for example, moved most of the pumice produced in the Surtsey eruption to the shores of Reykjanes peninsula in the south-western part of Iceland.

Similarly, one would expect diaspores to reach Surtsey by ocean transport from the eastern coast of Iceland or from the islands farther to the east. The currents may have a speed of over 7 km per day at the surface; thus it would only take two and a half days for the transport of a diaspore from Heimaey to Surtsey, a distance of 18 km in a straight line if the current headed directly that way. The ocean currents, however, are not the only forces affecting the transportation of objects on the sea surface, as this is also highly influenced by wind.

During the summer of 1967 an experiment was performed in order to demonstrate the drift which might take place from Heimaey. A few million plastic grains 2–4 mm in diameter were released into the sea from that island and an observation made of the drift. The winds shifted several times during this period and were not always favourable for the drift to Surtsey, but finally one week later a few hundred grains reached the island. The grains had thus drifted at the speed of 2.5 km per day.

Theoretically, diaspores transported by ocean fall off the edges of the source island, whence they float and drift away in all directions radiating from the source island until their drift is intercepted by an obstacle such as the shore of Surtsey. Should the diaspores float long enough the chances of reaching the shore of Surtsey can be expressed as the proportion between the Surtsey sector S and the total circumference of a ring with a centre in the source island and the distance between the islands as the radius R or

$$\frac{S}{2\pi R}$$

The amount of diaspores falling off the source island depends on its shore and whether this is evenly vegetated all around the island. The amount also depends on the type of vegetation, on weather, season and probably on a number of other factors, but mainly it depends on the circumference of the source island. It can be expressed as $2\pi r$ supposing the islands were circular with a radius r. A successful drift D would be affected by both these factors and could be expressed as

$$D = \frac{S}{2\pi R} \cdot 2\pi r = \frac{Sr}{R}$$

Table 18.1. Calculated chances for a diaspore to disperse by ocean to Surtsey

Islands closest to Surtsey	Area (sq. km)	Distance from Surtsey (km)	Calculated relative dispersal chances	Number of vascular species
Geirfuglasker	0.02	5.1	23	4
Súlnasker	0.04	11.6	14	7
Hellisey	0.13	15.0	18	9
Brandur	0.10	16.7	16	11
Álsey	0.25	17.0	25	25
Sudurey	0.20	18.3	20	23
Heimaey	16.0	21.6	236	150

The calculated chances of drift from the various islands near Surtsey is shown in Table 18.1. The drift value from Heimaey is the highest, which could indicate the great effect of its vegetation as a source material for Surtsey colonists. It must, however, be borne in mind that diaspores gradually sink as they drift and their exact floating ability is not known. Some species may float from Heimaey to Surtsey; others may never reach that far.

Similarly, the arrival of airborne organisms on Surtsey is affected by the air movement in the area or the weather conditions in the North Atlantic. Whenever a strong migration of birds or butterflies and moths was noted on Surtsey, it could be demonstrated by the aid of weather maps that conditions had been favourable for flight from central Europe or the British Isles to Iceland. And by the same way it could be shown that following northern winds in southern Iceland an increased number of Diptera and other flying insects could be collected on Surtsey. During such conditions there might be sunshine and calm weather on the southern lowland, but stronger winds out by the Westman Islands. The insects flying on the mainland in fair weather may be caught by this stronger air current and passively brought in flight out to the islands (Tables 18.2 and 18.3).

A passive flight of insects from the islands to Surtsey, as well as the transport of airborne seed, would be affected by the area of the source island rather than the circumference, and the chances of reaching Surtsey could be expressed as

$$D_{\text{air}} = \frac{Sr^2}{2R}$$

During the ten years of Surtsey's existence a large number of organisms have been observed on the island. Most of these organisms have been accidental migrants or visitors that have had little chance of survival in the rather hostile habitat of the dryland. These organisms have mostly dispersed from the adjacent landmasses, which in addition to the lush vegetation also have an abundant population of invertebrates and birds.

As these landmasses vary in size and distance from Surtsey, as well as in composition of flora and fauna, it is natural that their biotas do not all influence the colonisation of Surtsey to the same extent. The chance of dispersal is directly proportional to the number of species and size of population of the donating landmass and inversely proportional to its distance from Surtsey.

The special ability of the various life forms to disperse also plays a major role in the colonisation. The most mobile or the most tolerant animals have a better chance than others to move by air or water, and plants with buoyant

Table 18.2. *Terrestrial invertebrates found on Surtsey and the adjacent land*
(By courtesy of Lindroth *et al.* 1973).

Group	Mainland*			Heimaey	Small Westm. Isl.	Surtsey	Total
	I	II	III				
Diptera	145	116	15	135	60	105	231
Siphonaptera	—	3	—	—	—	1	4
Hymenoptera	95	80	4	77	34	8	138
Coleoptera	96	96	66	90	33	3	116
Lepidoptera	35	37	16	27	4	8	49
Trichoptera	7	5	2	1	—	1	8
Neuroptera	—	1	—	2	—	1	2
Hemiptera	33	24	3	34	7	2	48
Thysanoptera	4	1	—	5	4	—	5
Phthiraptera	—	5	—	3	—	1	9
Psocoptera	3	2	—	5	—	—	6
Plecoptera	1	1	—	—	—	—	1
Odonata	1	1	—	—	—	—	1
Thysanura	1	—	1	1	1	—	1
Protura	1	—	—	1	—	—	1
Collembola	46	14	—	39	25	6	59
Araneae	36	33	9	28	13	5	54
Opiliones	4	1	1	2	1	—	4
Chelonethi	1	—	—	1	—	—	1
Acari	210	37	—	149	88	17	279
Chilopoda	4	3	2	4	—	—	5
Diplopoda	1	—	—	3	—	—	3
Oniscoidea	3	2	1	2	1	—	3
Mollusca Gastropoda	22	16	4	16	8	—	24
Oligochaeta Lumbricidae	6	3	2	6	4	—	8
Turbellaria Terrestria	1	—	—	—	—	—	1
Total	736	482	126	631	287	158	1061

* The mainland is divided into three areas which are classified as I, II and III on the map shown in Figure 17.1.

Table 18.3. Occurrence of the different forms of Collembola on the Westman Islands (By courtesy of Lindroth et al. 1973).

	S. Iceland, Distr. I	Heimaey	Ellioaey	Bjarnarey	Suourey	Álfsey	Brandur	Hellisey	Súlnasker	Geirfuglasker	Surtsey
Total number of forms per area	49	45	8	15	18	12	8	3	6	5	8
Folsomia fimetaria	×	×	—	—	—	—	—	—	—	×	×
Onychiurus duplopunctatus	×	—	—	—	—	—	—	—	—	×	×
Archisotoma besselsi	×	×	—	—	—	—	—	—	—	—	×
Isotoma maritima	—	×	—	—	×	—	—	—	—	×	×
Hypogastrura assimilis	—	×	—	—	—	—	—	—	—	—	×
Vertagopus arborea	—	—	—	×	—	—	—	—	—	—	×
Anurida granaria	—	—	—	—	—	—	—	—	—	—	×
Proisotoma minuta	—	—	—	—	—	—	—	—	—	—	×
Onychiurus arm. pseudovanderdr.	×	×	×	×	×	×	—	—	—	×	
Anurida immsiana	—	×	×	—	×	—	—	—	—	×	
Isotoma viridis	×	×	×	×	×	×	×	×	×		
Hypogastrura purpurescens	×	×	—	×	×	×	×	×	×		
Folsomia quadrioculata	×	×	×	×	×	×	×	×	×		
Onychiurus arm. macfadyeni	—	—	—	—	×	×	×	×	×		
Xenylla humicola	—	—	—	—	×	×	×	—	×		
Friesea claviseta	—	—	—	—	—	—	—	—	×		
Lepidocyrtus lanuginosus	×	×	—	×	×	×	×	×			
Hypogastrura denticulata	×	×	×	×	×	×	×				
Sminthurinus aureus	×	×	—	×	×	—	×				
Sminthurides pumilis	×	×	—	—	—	—	×				
Tetracanthella arctica	×	×	×	—	×	×					
Isotomiella minor	×	×	×	×	—	×					
Onychiurus arm. campatus	×	×	—	×	×	×					
O. arm. bicampatus	×	×	—	—	×	×					
Lepidocyrtus cyaneus	×	×	—	—	—	×					
Friesea mirabilis	×	×	—	×	×						
Isotoma notabilis	×	×	—	×	×						
Onychiurus arm. armatus	×	×	—	—	×						
Pseudisotoma sensibilis	×	×	—	—	×						
Entomobrya nivalis	×	×	—	—	×						
Isotoma violacea	×	×	×	×							
Tullbergia krausbaueri	×	×	—	×							
Bourletiella hortensis	×	×	—	×							
Micranurida pygmaea	×	—	×								
Hypogastrura ripperi	×	×									
Willemia anophthalma	×	×									
Xenyllodes armatus	×	×									
Neanura muscorum	×	×									
Onychiurus arm. procampatus	×	×									
Tullbergia affinis	×	×									
Pseudanurophorus binoculatus	×	×									
Folsomia brevicauda	×	×									

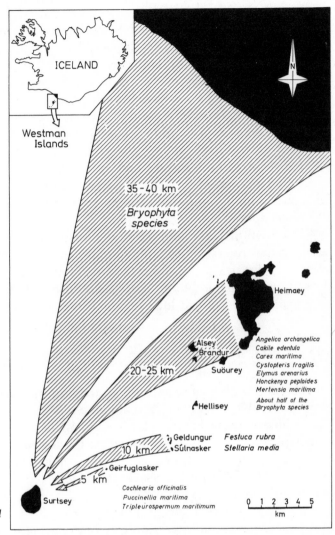

Figure 18.1. Possible dispersal of diaspores by air

and light seeds or spores are more readily transported by ocean currents and winds than heavy seeds.

The Surtsey study has shown that the island is subject to showers of airborne micro-organisms that continuously fall on its surface. Spores of mosses are also apparently carried to the island in large quantities, rather from the extensive moss fields of the mainland than from the small moss colonies of the neighbouring islands (Figure 18.1). However, the possibility of transportation of the vegetative parts of moss, although much heavier than spores, cannot be overlooked, as this is a frequent means of spreading of moss over lava flows on the mainland.

The vascular plants so far transported to Surtsey are almost exclusively coastal species obviously carried by ocean currents or brought in by birds from the neighbouring shores. Surtsey being an island with a sandy fore-shore and the neighbouring land masses having a highly maritime vegetation increases the possibility of dispersal of such coastal plants, whereas plants from sources farther away have less chance of dispersal. An exception to this priority of coastal species is the transport of seeds of plants carried down by the rivers on the mainland. Seeds having the best floating ability and retaining germination ability after immersion in ocean water are most capable of successful transport and survival.

Another exception is the transport of seeds of inland plants that have been picked up by birds and brought to the island. These introductions are also rather sporadic.

As far as animals are concerned, the lower organisms of the smallest size and greatest tolerance to unfavourable environments have shown the greatest ability for successful transport. Flying insects and birds have also proved quite capable of air dispersal to Surtsey, whereas soil animals and land mammals have had little or no chance of dispersal to the island.

THE SUCCESSIONS

Of the vast number of species so far arriving on Surtsey, only a very few have been able to establish themselves. Many spores and seeds have germinated without further success of growth, and consumers have found a negligible amount of food sources on the island to survive on. For most of the organisms attempting colonisation it has been a hard struggle for existence. Although the dispersal has been quite restricted, the highly special-ised and stringent environmental conditions present on Surtsey have chiefly governed strict natural selection of pioneers.

An unfavourable substrate could be one reason for a slow colonisation on an island. But the substrate on Surtsey *per se* does not seem to differ markedly from other volcanic tephra, and plants can grow on it where water is available.

This was demonstrated by moving three types of substrates, e.g. tuff, sea sand and pumice, from Surtsey and placing them in containers $35 \times 55 \times 18$ cm in size with five other substrates in the middle of a meadowland at an experimental station near Reykjavík. After three summers the surface of a peat sample had obtained 60.7% cover of vascular plants that had blown in as diaspores from the neighbourhood, whereas the Surtsey substrate had a 10% average cover and some cinder from the Hekla eruption in 1970 only obtained 1.9% cover (Table 18.4).

Table 18.4. *Colonisation of vascular plants on various substrates placed in a meadow on the mainland*

| Species | Mean cover | | | | | | Old sea sand | Peat |
| | From Hekla 1970 | | | From Surtsey | | | | |
	Ash	Pumice	Cinder	Sand	Pumice	Tuff		
Pteriodophyta								
Equisetum arvense								0.2
Monocotyledoneae								
Agrostis canina	7.8			0.6	7.8	3.0		3.4
Agrostis stolonifera	5.3							
Agrostis tenuis					1.3			
Deschampsia caespitosa								14.0
Festuca rubra			1.8				0.1	
Festuca vivipara	0.5	0.2	13.8	8.5	1.0	0.4	1.8	23.0
Luzula multiflora			0.8					3.3
Luzula spicata								8.0
Luzula sp.	0.6	0.5		0.4	0.6	0.4		0.3
Poa glauca						0.8		
Poa pratensis								0.2
Dicotyledoneae								
Arenaria norvegica							0.2	
Armeria maritima							0.6	
Cerastium alpinum		0.1					0.1	6.0
Cerastium caespitosum	0.1	1.0		0.8	0.4	3.4	2.0	
Galium normanii							0.3	
Polygonum viviparum		0.1					0.1	
Rumex acetosa							0.6	
Rumex acetosella				0.6				
Sagina nodosa						0.6		
Thymus drucei	0.3	0.1			0.2	0.1	1.1	1.7
Total cover	14.5	1.9	16.4	10.9	11.3	8.65	6.2	60.7

The environment on Surtsey is cool, windy and rainy, but the periodical drought is mostly responsible for the slow establishment of life on the island. As the tephra gradually hardens into tuff, its water-retention will increase and the abrasive effect of the glass particles will be minimised. This substratum will then be accessible to mosses and even grasses and to various dicotyledonous species now growing on the neighbouring islands.

The xeric habitats of the lava flows were rather suddenly colonised by mosses following a five-year initiation period. When the local individuals of moss started reproducing, there was a population explosion in the habitat and the colonisation became quite rapid. During the succeeding three years the mosses spread over most of the lava that had a suitable environment and was not too much affected by the salt spray. This enormous increase in distribution may be measured in number of quadrats occupied by moss (*see* Figure 14.13). In 1967 moss was found only in three quadrats, the figure had jumped to 120 quadrats in 1971. Since then the tufts of moss are gradually enlarging and uniting in a close mat, and the biomass per unit area is increasing. The moss invaded the lava as a monoculture.

The secondary invaders, bacteria, algae and moulds, may now be found associated with the moss, but the moss does not seem to rely on them in its establishment on the lava. By comparing the xerarch succession of the vegetational development on the lava flows of the mainland, it may be assumed that the Surtsey moss will develop a thick continuous carpet, at least in the centre of the lava apron. This moss carpet will then collect dust and minerals, and nutrients will be deposited in the dead mat of moss rhizoids which will form a layer of humus in the juvenile soil. The accumulation of humus will then cause moisture to be retained on the lava surface. The pioneer lichens will occupy the higher ridges of the lava and gradually corrode its surface, providing better anchorage for other plants. This primary succession of moss and lichen will provide a suitable habitat for higher plants which then, in turn, will invade the lava area. Gradually a heath vegetation with the sedge, *Carex rigida*, the crowberry, *Empetrum nigrum*, and low-growing willows, *Salix* species, may invade the moss carpet in the most sheltered areas. But it is highly unlikely that the island will ever obtain a climax vegetation of birch as the lava flows of the mainland, because of the frequent salt spray and the heavy storms.

SURTSEY AND OTHER ISLANDS

The biota of Surtsey has been compared to that of the other members of the Westman Islands and, although it is situated farther to the south, the climate does not differ enough to cause the Surtsey biota to deviate markedly from those of the other islands, but its biota will show a pronounced difference when compared to the biota of the island of Grímsey, which is situated off the northern coast of Iceland. These two islands are the extreme outposts of Iceland, Grímsey being in the Arctic Ocean and Surtsey in the Atlantic.

The Grímsey biota is Arctic and has been transported over the Arctic Ocean, whereas the Surtsey biota is more European and is transported over the Atlantic. These are similarly the routes by which the biota has in general been carried to Iceland after the country had been freed from the ice dome some ten to twenty thousand years ago. Although Surtsey is small, in comparison to Iceland, the island may represent its southern part and the same principles of dispersal and colonisation are involved. Surtsey has both the lava flows and tuff mountains that are common on the mainland, with vegetations which have undergone much the same successional steps that are now starting to develop on Surtsey. The southern coast of Iceland has an extensive low sandy shore open to the Atlantic and is susceptible to the debris carried by the Gulf Stream.

The shore of the northern ness on Surtsey is similarly subject to various drifts from the same ocean current. Although this coastal strip of Surtsey is small in comparison with that of the mainland, it is already occupied by an unusually high number of coastal species of the Icelandic flora. This indicates that the number of coastal species increases only slightly with the size of an island. It seems that an island, which has reached a certain minimal size, can actually support all coastal species available in the area, and Surtsey is definitely large enough to do this. The lagoon which originally existed on the northern ness added to the diversity of the coastal habitat. The fresh-water containers also served as attractions for birds and these became the centres of colonisation. Fresh-water reservoirs on an island markedly increase diversity in the habitats and add to the number of possible colonising species. It has been suggested that ocean islands cannot maintain a fresh-water reservoir if they are less than one hectare in area. Although Surtsey is considerably larger, it is doubtful that fresh water will collect on the island to any extent. There are hardly any fresh water deposits either on the other islands in the Westman Islands group. This is due to the poor water-holding ability of the volcanic substratum, a common phenomenon on all volcanic islands.

Biotas of volcanic islands may differ due to climatic differences, remoteness, diversity of available species of the source region, age, size and physiography. In spite of this difference, many of the same principles are involved affecting transport of potential immigrants and their colonisation.

In the Atlantic one may compare the biota of various volcanic islands from north to south along the Atlantic ridge, such as: Jan Mayen, Iceland, Azores, and Tristan da Cunha. These islands show a marked difference in types and number of species and number of endemics, but they have in common the relative poverty of species, lack of genetic diversity in the present taxa and ecological disharmony when compared with the biota of adjacent continents.

Of the 450 species of flowering plants found in Iceland there are hardly any true endemics, nor of the 45 species of Jan Mayen, whereas there are 15 endemics of the 124 species of flowering plants of Tristan da Cunha. These are all remote islands that reach an altitude of over 2000 m. They vary in size and although the diversity of the biota of an island is, in general, directly proportional to its area, this trend is not as effective on the biota as the climate may be. Jan Mayen is 371.8 sq. km in size, compared with the 159 sq. km of the Tristan group, and has only one third of the number of vascular plants. These islands may be of similar age or less than 20 million years old, but the actual age of the biota is highly different, as the North Atlantic islands have undergone denudations during glacial periods. Thus their present biota only dates back to the end of the last ice age, which explains their lack of endemics.

One of the factors influencing the formation of endemic species is the founder effect, where a small number of colonists on an island will contribute only a fraction of the gene pool of the source population and the random samples of migrants may not have represented the original population in genetic respects. This initial difference may result in an endemic species after an evolution of 10 million years (in Tristan) or over 10 thousand years (in Iceland), but the tendency towards genetic drift will hardly be measurable on a 10-year old island. Nevertheless, the first individual of flowering plants, such as the pioneer of scurvy grass which has now started growth on Surtsey, may have a much greater influence on the population than possible later arrivals. The majority or even all individuals of the future population of this species on the island may descend from this particular individual. But there will hardly occur a chance loss of many alleles in the genetic constitution of the Surtsey population of this particular species. This would be effective if the island were more remote. But chances are that many other individuals will arrive later and level out the possibility of much genetic difference in the species.

Similarly, the migrant species may not be a random sample of the species in the neighbouring community. A chance migration of a rare species might thus affect the formation of an unusual association. This, however, is not the case on Surtsey, as nearly all the colonists are either very common in the neighbourhood or in comparative habitats on the mainland such as new lava flows or sandy beaches. The colonisation of the first mosses may have been somewhat unusual, but soon the most common moss species of lava flows in Iceland also dominated the Surtsey lava.

Following the establishment of a colonist and its first successful reproduction on the island, the distribution of the species in the ecosystem enters a new phase. From then on the spread of the species is subject to two modes of distribution. One is an external migration, which follows a relatively stable pattern year by year. The other is based on an internal source of diaspores, becoming increasingly effective as time goes on and succeeding generations start reproducing and forming new centres of distributions. The internal migration is characterised by a radiant spread of organisms from the source plant, forming colonies with varying density according to their processes of dissemination and vegetative reproduction. In the Surtsey research, individual plants have been mapped to keep track of this basic development, and the structure of the vegetation as is demonstrated by the following examples.

It usually takes a *Honckenya* plant three years to reach the state of flowering. In 1971 the first five plants of this species developed flowers and one matured seeds and bore two fruits. The following year 12 plants flowered, of which 9 matured and produced 346 fruits. The seeds from both years were mostly distributed in the neighbourhood of the flowering plants, some were buried deep in sand and others carried out to sea.

In 1973 there were 548 plants of this species recorded on Surtsey, of which 100 to 150 may be assumed to have developed from seaborne seed, whereas the rest, or some 400 plants, grew from locally produced seeds.

Similarly, plants of the species *Cochlearia officinalis* have flowered since 1971 and produced a number of seeds. This continued in 1972, and in 1973 four plants became seed producers.

In studying the reproduction of a flowering pioneer plant on the virgin substrate of Surtsey, one may take as an example the *Cochlearia* plant No. 70–74 in quadrat N 13, which flowered and produced seeds in 1971. The following summer 90 seeds germinated and produced new offspring, which occupied the space within a radius of 1 m around the mother-plant. Ten of these plants died during the same summer and some more died during the following winters. Still others were crowded out during the summer of 1973, so that only 43 individuals of this generation survived in the autumn of 1973. The mother plant did not produce seed in 1972, but in 1973 seed production was again abundant and seven seeds germinated and grew already in the autumn. Thus there were 50 offsprings of two generations surviving from this single mother plant in three years. A colony was established, which displayed many of the major ecological problems to which living beings are subject in the environment, such as competition for space between individuals and for their use of available energy, nutrition and water. This pioneer population also showed variation in distribution and density, as well as fluctuation in the annual reproduction rate and mortality (Figure 18.2).

The development of the sedge, *Carex maritima*, may on the other hand be taken as an example of the establishment of a colony by vegetative propagation. The species is common on the sands and volcanic soils of the southern mainland, whence diaspores may have been brought to Surtsey by geese that feed on this species. A single plant started growth in 1970, quite isolated in quadrat M 11 on the central part of the island where the substrate was sand-filled lava. In 1972 it had begun to propagate by rhizomes, and in the summer of 1973 11 propagules were formed. The distribution of the individuals in this colony is restricted by the length of rhizomes. Thus the area occupied by the new population was much smaller than that formed through seed distribution, or only 13 × 18 cm (Figure 18.3). When the daughter plants in turn start propagating, their offspring will not enjoy the

Cochlearia officinalis (no. 70-74)
schematic drawing of sexual propagation

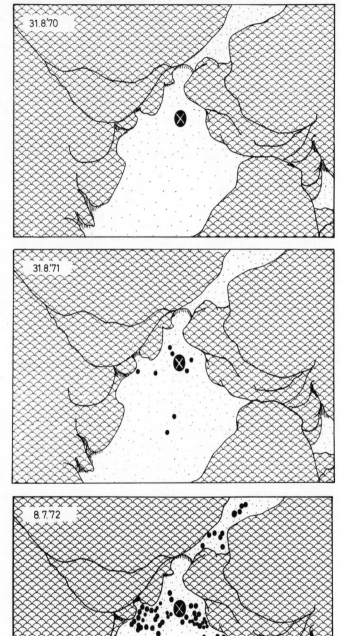

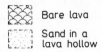
Bare lava
Sand in a
lava hollow

Plate 19. A young gannet, one of the inhabitants on Súlnasker, an old volcanic island in the neighbourhood of Surtsey, looks over the strait at a future nesting ground

Plate 20. The author on Surtsey, 18 August 1966. Early next morning a fissure opened near this very spot

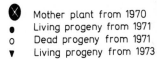

X   Mother plant from 1970
●   Living progeny from 1971
○   Dead progeny from 1971
▼   Living progeny from 1973

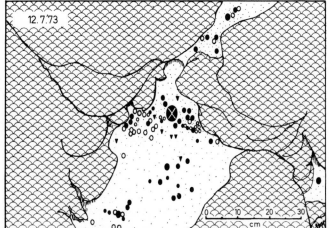

Figure 18.2. The population increase in scurvy grass, Cochlearia officinalis

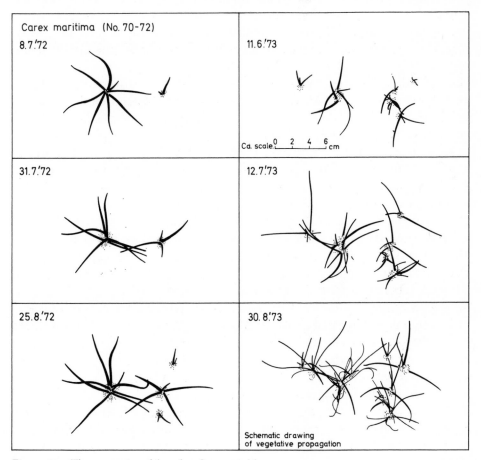

Figure 18.3. The propagation of the sedge, Carex maritima

same freedom of space and there will be an increased and an uneven competition between individuals of the population.

The difference in climate of remote volcanic islands greatly affects their biota. Thus a very low precipitation such as that of Lanzarote, the easternmost member of the Canary Islands, accounts for a slow rate of introduction of plants to its basaltic lava flow in comparison with the colonising rate of the Surtsey lava affected by the high humidity.

When high humidity is also accompanied by high temperatures, the colonisation can be quite rapid as in the case of the island of Krakatoa, which became almost completely denuded of life during the explosive eruption in 1883. Fourteen years following the eruption there were 50 species of vascular plants growing on the island. There were numerous coastal plants and several had spread to higher elevations. It has been estimated that 60% had been transported by sea, 32% by air currents and 8% by birds. But only 25 years after the outbreak the island was again covered with a thick vegetation and had obtained an animal population comparable to that of the neighbouring archipelago. The dispersal and colonisation was so rapid that three years after the eruption it was too late to investigate how all the different life forms had managed to disperse and colonise the island. In contrast, the low temperature on Surtsey makes the colonisation a very slow process that can be followed in detail from year to year. Thus, the transportation route has often been definitely demonstrated, and in that way it has been possible to prove that seeds of higher plants may be carried to the island by various means on sea surface, by floats, by wind and by birds; and that spores of mosses, lichens and ferns are mostly windborne. Based on the study of Krakatoa, it has been taken for granted that blue–green algae are the first colonisers of a volcanic substratum, followed by lichens and moss and then higher plants. But the Surtsey study shows that many of the coastal species occupied the lava flows as pioneers independent of any lower plants, and that the mosses arrived a few years later, although they eventually became the most active colonisers of the lava. A similar phenomenon takes place on Hawaii, where the *Metrosideros collina* is one of the first trees to occupy the new lava, spreading its roots over its surface even before mosses arrive.

In general, the biota of an island is in a state equilibrium when governed by the balance between immigration and extinction. The immigration rate may be high where the distance to the island is short and where there is an abundant source of species.

On Surtsey the immigration rate has been very slow compared with that of Krakatoa and many years will pass before it reaches equilibrium. An exception is the moss flora, which had a sudden and rapid rate of immigration. This may be demonstrated by a sharp sloping curve obtained when the distribution is plotted against time. A curve which already started to level off in 1971. More remote in time is a possible extinction of species from Surtsey. This may take place when the lava becomes completely covered with grasses succeeding the pioneer mosses and lichens and has developed a heavy carpet of red fescue, preventing growth of most other higher plants. This in turn will be excavated by puffins or again denuded by the rich guano deposits of the gannets, which may eventually colonise Surtsey as the neighbouring islands. Finally, the shores may erode to the same extent as those of Súlnasker, cutting away the low sandy beaches and transforming the coast into the steep cliffs so common on the outer islands. This takes place simultaneously with an extinction of the coastal plants that so far have been the main immigrants of higher plants on Surtsey.

In sand-covered parts the lyme-grass is a pioneer species. It develops by stolons and collects the blowing sand until a dune is formed. A minute dune formation is already taking place on the island. Later, red fescue, *Festuca rubra*, will enter into the stand of lyme-grass and stabilise the dune with other low-growing grasses.

On the sand and gravelly beach the coastal plants are increasing in number and will expand over most of the upper part of the ness. There the oyster-plant, *Mertensia*, and sea-rocket, *Cakile*, are the pioneers of the shingle beach vegetation.

The advancement of the coastal plants towards the lava has been such that it now merges with the moss carpet. There it is forming a transition zone on the border of beach and lava. Ten years after the formation of Surtsey the pioneers of mosses and higher plants are growing together, actively forming an association of a partially fixed dune vegetation with the sea-sandwort, *Honckenya peploides*, as the dominant species.

Exposed to the sea on the south side, a community is being developed that will form the cliff vegetation with chickweed, *Stellaria media*, and the scurvy-grass, *Cochlearia officinalis*, as pioneer species. The angelica so far found only on the northern ness may later join these two species to form clusters of growth on the shelves on the southern cliffs.

The pioneer species of flora and fauna that have so far established themselves on Surtsey are all common inhabitants of the neighbourhood. Thus the island's biotic community being only a fraction of the Westman Islands' biota may to some extent be considered to be in harmony with the biota of the adjacent land masses.

In forecasting future trends in the biotic development it is, however, reasonable to predict that the biota may become more variable on Surtsey than on many other members of the Westman Islands, due to its greater size and diversity in topography.

Many of the Westman Islands are mere stacks with sheer cliffs, whereas Surtsey has low beaches. The Surtsey coasts will, however, steadily erode and high sea cliffs will eventually be formed similar to those found on its neighbouring islands. The cliffs will serve as breeding places for various birds; fulmars, *Fulmarus glacialis*, and kittiwakes, *Rissa tridactyle*, or razorbill, *Alca torda*, and black guillemot, *Cepphus grylle*, while the grass-covered slopes will be occupied by the puffin, *Fratercula arctica*, and finally, on the summits, colonies may be established by the stately gannet, *Sula bassana*, the queen of the outer islands (Plate 19).

REFERENCES

BACKER, C. A., *The Problem of Krakatao as seen by a Botanist*, Martinus Nijhoff, the Hague, 299 (1929)
LINDROTH, C. H., ANDERSSON, H., BÖDVARSSON, H. and RICHTER, S., *Surtsey, Iceland, Entomologica Scandinavica Supplementum*, 5, Munksgaard, Copenhagen, 280 (1973)
STEINDÓRSSON, S., Flora Grímseyjar, *J. Icelandic Botany*, 89–94 (1954)
STEINDÓRSSON, S., 'Jan Mayen', *Náttúrufr.*, **28**, 57–89 (1958)
WACE, N. M. and DICKSON, J. H., 'The terrestrial botany of the Tristan da Cunha Islands', *Phil. Trans. Royal Soc. London Series B. Biol. Sci.*, 759, **249**, 273–360 (1965)

19

ACKNOWLEDGEMENT

The subject of this book particularly concerns the study of terrestrial life on the island of Surtsey during the first 10 years of the island's existence. In 1964 I had decided to try to follow the first steps of the colonisation of life on the island and the possible succession of communities (Plate 20).

To render this possible the U. S. Atomic Energy Commission in Washington granted financial aid and the Commission has generously supported these studies ever since. Although I originally started studying the development of life on the island and have partly continued the research for the past 10 years, the results presented here are nevertheless based on the work of several scientists from various disciplines whose valuable investigations have broadened the general knowledge of these natural phenomena.

These scientific results have, in general, appeared in the *Surtsey Research Progress Reports*, published by the Surtsey Research Society, which has, from the start, been presided over by Steingrimur Hermannsson, Director of the Icelandic Research Council. In this book I have chosen to summarise some of the various results obtained from this research work without directly quoting each time the name of the scientist and author concerned, but I have listed the references at the end of each chapter. This should facilitate further reading of the original study.

In summing up the work done over the last 10 years I have considered it appropriate to start relating the geological history of Surtsey and the Westman Islands in general. The main sources of information in these chapters have been obtained from the Icelandic geologists Gudmundur Kjartansson, Sigurdur Thorarinsson, Thorleifur Einarsson and Sveinn Jakobsson. Furthermore, I have used the results of geophysical research carried out by Gudmundur Sigvaldason and Trausti Einarsson. J. O. Norrmann from Sweden has mostly performed studies of the topographical changes on the island, to which I refer in the book. The oceanographic research has been done by Unnsteinn Stefánsson and Svend-Aage Malmberg, while the meteorological research has been led by Hlynur Sigtryggsson, Director of the Meteorological Office of Iceland. Several biologists visited Surtsey and added to our knowledge of the colonisation of life on the island. C. Ponnamperuma has carried out biochemical research whereas R. Young, T. D. Brock, W. Schwartz and Arinbjörn Kolbeinsson have been responsible for the bacteriological research. Sigurdur Jonsson and Sigurdur Hallsson have studied the marine algae, while G. H. Schwabe has been occupied with the dryland algae. Hördur Kristinsson has studied lichens and Bergthor Johannsson has supervised the classification of mosses found on the island. Eythor Einarsson has compared the colonisation of vascular plants growing on Surtsey with that on nunataks on the Vatna-jökull glacier. C. H. Lindroth led the enthymological work, his co-workers being: H. Anderson and Högm Bödvarsson, and further collection of insects has been made by Sigurdur Richter, Hálfdán Björnsson, Erlingur Ólafsson and others.

Adalsteinn Sigurdsson and W. Nicolaisen carried out marine biological studies around Surtsey. Finnur Gudmundsson supervised the observation of birds and other ornothological research work.

The main part of this book, however, is a report of my studies as well as those of my assistants, who have done most of the routine field work on which are based the vegetation maps and various floral lists.

I am particularly grateful to my assistants for their contribution to the Surtsey research. Without their skilful observations and their expedient means of tackling new problems under often highly difficult circumstances this work would not have been accomplished. The study of the vegetation of the outer islands benefited greatly from Björn Johnsen's knowledge of the local area, and the chapter on this research work is mainly based on our article in *Greinar* **4**, No 3 (1967) published by the Societas Scientiarum Islandica. Further studies on vegetation and various other biological work was carried out by the following assistants: Sigurdur Helgason, Sigurdur Richter, Águst Bjarnason, Bjartmar Sveinbjörnsson, Ragnar Jónasson and Skúli Magnússon. I am very much indebted to Skúli Magnússon for his part in the bryological research. The mosses play a major role in the colonisation of Surtsey and therefore a thorough investigation of these plants is of major importance for our knowledge of the development of the ecosystem of Surtsey. It is with his approval that some of the results of the work are published in this book. Furthermore, Skúli Magnússon has drawn most of the maps, for which I am grateful as well as for being allowed to present some of his photographs. Most of the pictures were, however, taken by the author. These pictures are nevertheless only a fraction of the myriads of existing photographs from the eruption and the islands. Several films have also been produced, the most renowned being those of Osvaldur Knudsen.

I am also indebted to the Agricultural Research Institute and the Surtsey Research Society for various assistance rendered in connection with this research.

Many persons and organisations are to be thanked for the smooth transportation to the island, but especially the Icelandic Coast Guard, which at the start of the eruption provided willing and useful assistance to scientists. The construction of the scientists' hut has greatly improved research facilities on the island. This hut has been nicknamed Pálsbaer (Paul's farm) in honour of Professor Paul S. Bauer of the American University in Washington DC, who has shown great interest in the Surtsey research and in various ways supported the work done there.

The terrestrial research would not have been as detailed as it is if it had not been for the generous support of the United States Atomic Energy Commission. And I am particularly grateful to Dr. John H. Wolfe for the enthusiasm and inspiring attitude he has shown in regard to this project.

When I had written the major part of this book on Surtsey a new eruption took place on Heimaey. As it affected life in the area I have consequently included a short chapter on this event. Many of the Icelandic scientists that witnessed the eruption of Surtsey also investigated the volcanic activities on Heimaey, among these were the earth scientists Thorbjörn Sigurgeirsson and Thorleifur Einarsson. Using their knowledge and experience, which to some extent was acquired from the Surtsey eruption, the engineers tackled the advancing lava of Heimaey that threatened to totally destroy the town. By constructing ramparts and cooling the lava by constantly pumping sea-water on its molten edge it was possible to avoid a major destruction of the town. This would hardly have been accomplished if a similar cooling operation had not been tried previously on Surtsey on a small scale.

I have attempted to present a description of the rather dramatic eruption of Surtsey and to review the parts played by the various organisms in colonisation of the island by giving a brief outline of the geology and the biology of the surrounding stage. In my description of these events I have used as a background the Norse mythology, as it appears in the ancient Edda

poem *Völuspá*, and recited in the *Deluding of Gylfi* written by Snorri Sturluson (1179–1241). There is an apparent conformity in the Surtsey eruption
and the Nordic understanding of creation and development of life and land,
and it has previously been pointed out that the ancient authors very likely
were acquainted with, or had witnessed, submarine volcanic activities.

To me personally, the eruption of Surtsey and the events that followed—
the formation of new land and its gradual colonisation by life—has certainly
been a revelation. The display of these natural phenomena were so
magnificent, the powers of the elements both in constructing and demolish-
ing land so apparent, and the continuous struggle for the existence of life
so fundamental that they are bound to direct one's thoughts towards the
creative forces of the universe and to the origin and destiny of life.

INDEX

(References to Figures in bold type)